CUB SCOUT FUN BOOK

Boy Scouts of America

HOW TO USE THIS BOOK

Here is a book of projects Cub Scouts and Webelos Scouts like to do. You can do most of these projects alone with materials that you find around home. Sometimes a parent or other adult may need to help you.

When you do many of these activities, you will not only have fun, but you will also earn credit for achievements and electives in the *Wolf Cub Scout Book* and the *Big Bear Cub Scout Book,* or activity badges in the *Webelos Scout Book.*

33213
ISBN 0-8395-3213-X
©1986 Boy Scouts of America
Revised 1997

10 9 8 7 6 5 4 3 2 1

CONTENTS

ABBREVIATIONS

Some common abbreviations used in projects
are as follows:

QUANTITY

tsp.	=	teaspoon
tbsp.	=	tablespoon
c.	=	cup
pt.	=	pint
qt.	=	quart
oz.	=	ounce
lb.	=	pound
doz.	=	dozen

Nails are ordered by "penny" size.

d	=	"penny"

[Example: a fourpenny nail would be written "4d"]

DISTANCE

" or in.	=	inch
' or ft.	=	foot
yd.	=	yard
cm.	=	centimeter

TOOLS

HAMMERS

There are many different types of hammers. A bell-faced hammer has a rounded face that lets you drive nails all the way down to the surface of the wood without leaving hammer marks.

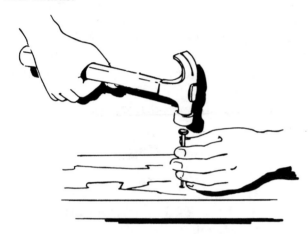

It is best to grip the handle of the hammer firmly right down by its end. Place the nail exactly in the spot where you want it to go in, and hold it in place while you *lightly* tap it with the hammer to get it started in the wood. Be sure to hit the nail squarely with the face of the hammer so the nail goes in straight. If the nail bends or goes in crooked, remove it and start again. When hammering small nails, avoid hitting your fingers by pushing the nails through a piece of light cardboard and holding the cardboard instead of the nail.

SCREWDRIVERS

There are two types of screwdrivers: one for slotted screws and one for Phillips-head screws. Always use the screwdriver that fits the size and type of the screw. The wrong size will often damage the slot in the screw or the blade of the screwdriver. Don't use a screwdriver that has a worn or chipped blade. Don't use your screwdriver to pry boards apart or to remove nails. Never hammer on the head of a screwdriver.

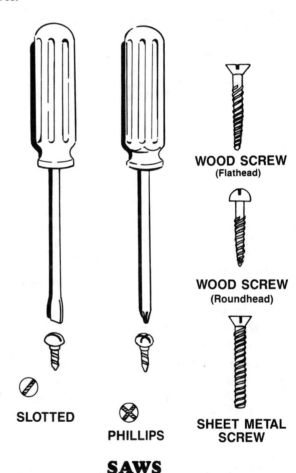

WOOD SCREW
(Flathead)

WOOD SCREW
(Roundhead)

**SHEET METAL
SCREW**

SLOTTED

PHILLIPS

SAWS

There are many different sizes and shapes of saws. Each one is suited for a different job. The crosscut saw is used for cutting across the grain and the ripsaw is used for cutting along the grain of the wood. The usual handsaw is a crosscut saw. It cuts on both the forward and backward strokes.

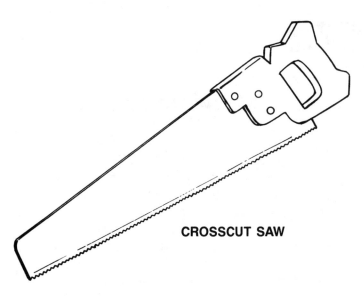

CROSSCUT SAW

The compass or keyhole saw is used for making internal cuts (holes) or for cutting in narrow places. The coping saw is used for cutting on curves.

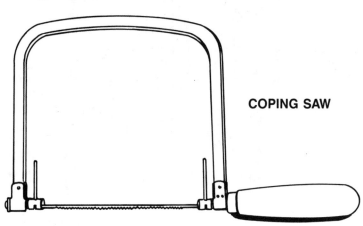

COPING SAW

Always start your cut on the board waste side of your cutting line.

After you have started, use long, easy strokes, moving the saw blade from tip to hilt. As you near the end of your cut, make sure you support the waste portion of the board so that it doesn't break off and leave a ragged edge.

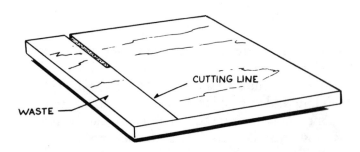

DRILLS

Drills are used for making small holes. There are push drills and rotary crank drills. Drill bits come in an assortment of sizes from $\frac{1}{64}$- to $\frac{1}{4}$-inch diameter that fit most drills. You may wish to make a "starter hole" for your drill bit with an awl or nail first. Make sure the bit is straight in the drill's chuck before you start drilling.

Use a brace and bit for making larger holes with auger bits. You can get a lot of leverage and cut through wood quickly and easily. Be sure to hold the brace straight. When the bit starts to break through the other side of the wood, turn your piece over and finish boring the hole from the other side.

This keeps the wood from splintering and splitting.

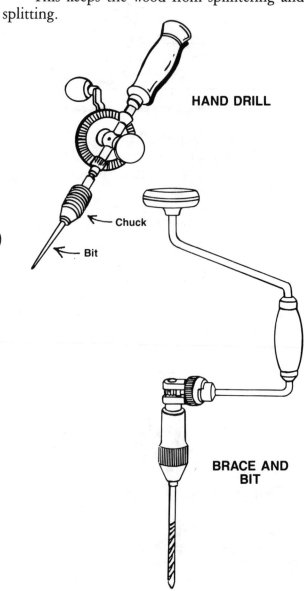

HAND DRILL

Chuck

Bit

BRACE AND BIT

C-CLAMP

A C-clamp is named for the shape of its frame. They come in a number of sizes. You will frequently use two or three at a time.

C-clamps are used to hold pieces of wood together for gluing, to hold your work in place, and to keep pieces from moving when you are boring holes.

To prevent a C-clamp from making a dent in your wood, place a thin piece of scrap wood between your good board and the clamps.

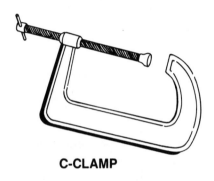

C-CLAMP

MEASURING AND MARKING

Several different types of measuring devices are available. Folding rules and steel tapes are good all-round measurers. Yardsticks made of wood are not always straight or accurate. When you want to make corners and straight edges, use a *square.* This has two pieces at right angles to each other and a thin steel blade.

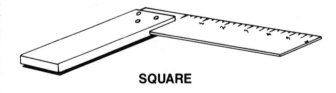

SQUARE

SANDPAPER AND SANDING

To smooth the ends of a cut board and the sides of your pieces, use sandpaper. Always sand *with* the wood's grain. Proper sanding will give your project a much better look and feel.

Sandpaper comes in various grades, from very rough to very fine grit. Always do your final sanding with a fine sandpaper and wipe off any dust with a cloth. This is especially important when you want to join two pieces of wood or to finish with a stain or paint.

SAFETY POINTERS

- Know how to use the tool before you start.

- Keep your work area neat.

- Never use a tool with a dull cutting edge, dull bit, or loose part.

- Use tools only for the jobs they are intended to do. Never use a screwdriver to pry or pound.

- Don't try to repair a tool yourself. Either get a new one or have an expert do the job.

HAVE FUN!

HOW TO ENLARGE A PATTERN

Patterns can be enlarged (or reduced) by using the "grid" method.

PROCEDURE

1. Put tracing paper over the design to be enlarged. Mark the design's outer limits.

2. Using these limits as guides, draw parallel horizontal and vertical lines on the paper to create a checkerboard or grid. If the pattern is small, make the lines ½ cm. apart; make them 1 cm. apart if your design is large.

3. Letter each top square. Number down the left side.

4. Tape the grid over the original drawing and trace a pattern onto the grid.

5. Decide how much of an enlargement is desired. Draw another grid with larger squares so the total width and length is the size of the finished enlargement. The large grid MUST have the same number of squares as the small grid.

6. Letter and number the new grid the same as the small grid.

7. Copy the drawing's lines into their exact position in each square of the large grid.

8. Now, transfer your newly enlarged pattern to your work surface (wood, cardboard, paper). Using carbon paper, trace the design with a blunt pencil.

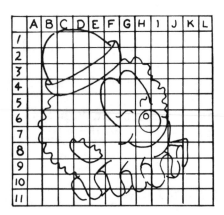

GLUE
TYPES AND USES

Always use the right type of glue for the project you are working on. Here are some tips:

★ SCHOOL PASTE is for pasting paper only. It doesn't always hold tight when dry.

★ WHITE GLUE is for paper, wood, cardboard, and ceramic. It will wash out of your clothes if you don't let it dry.

★ "TACKY" WHITE GLUE is for paper, wood, cardboard, foam, and styrofoam. This costs a little more than regular white glue, but a little goes a long way. Because it is "tacky," things stick together and hold much faster. Sometimes it is called craft glue.

★ RUBBER CEMENT is for paper. Paper can be repositioned. This is not a glue for permanent uses.

★ CONTACT CEMENT is for almost anything, including vinyl and plastics. Remember to coat each surface to be glued. Let the glue dry to the sticky stage and mash both sticky sides together. This forms a very permanent bond.

★ CLEAR SILICONE is for plastics. Use very small quantities.

★ WHEAT PASTE is for papier-mâchè.

★ EGG WHITE is a very lightweight "glue" for kites.

★ GLUE STICK is for paper and lightweight materials. It is also good for kites. Because it is in stick (solid) form, it is not messy to use.

TROPHY SKIN

Use the trophy skin to display extra badges you have earned and decorate your room.

MATERIALS

Two 18" sticks or dowels

Two 15" sticks or dowels

Four 12" pieces and one 90" piece of hemp twine

Four 12" pieces of bell wire

One 12" × 15" piece of thin vinyl

PROCEDURE

1. Bind the four sticks or dowels together with bell wire to form a rectangle. Be sure to make these joints as rigid and tight as possible.

2. Cut the piece of vinyl in the shape of a skin, following the pattern in the picture. Punch holes around the edges as indicated.

3. Tie the four corners in place with the four 12" pieces of twine. Then lace around the skin with the 90" piece of twine.

4. Your badges may be sewn, stapled, or glued to the skin.

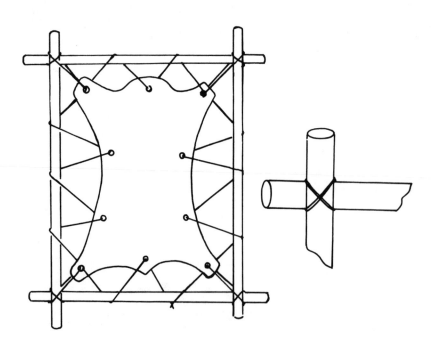

NECKERCHIEF SLIDES

Here are three ideas to get you started on your neckerchief slide collection.

ADVANCEMENT POSSIBILITY

Webelos Craftsman Activity Badge

WOODEN SLIDES

MATERIALS

Wood scraps, about ¼" thick

Sandpaper

Paint or stain, if desired

A piece of leather or vinyl ½"×2¾" (to staple or nail to back of slide)

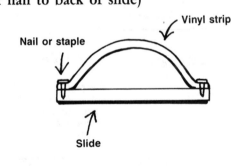

TREE BRANCH SLIDES

A "slice" of tree branch with the bark left on

Leather or vinyl strip ½"×2¾" (to staple or nail to back of slide)

Enamel paint

Varnish, shellac, or sealer

TREE BRANCH SLIDE

STOP SIGN

HAMMER

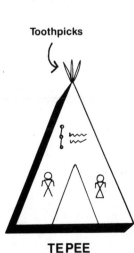

TEPEE

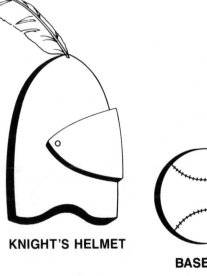

KNIGHT'S HELMET

BASEBALL

LEATHER OR VINYL SLIDES

Scraps of leather or vinyl in color to suit your "theme"

Permanent markers

Wiggly eyes or buttons for faces

Pipecleaners or vinyl strips for the back of the slide

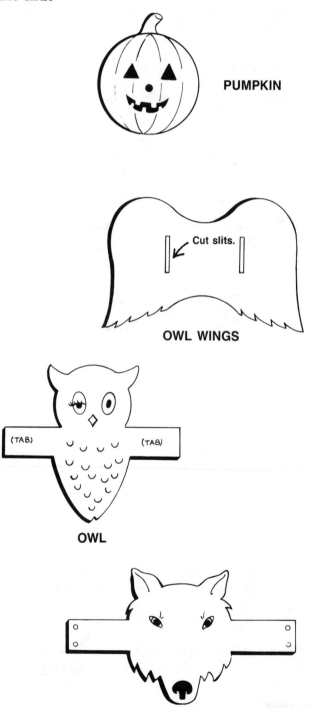

PUMPKIN

OWL WINGS

Cut slits.

(TAB) (TAB)

OWL

WOLF

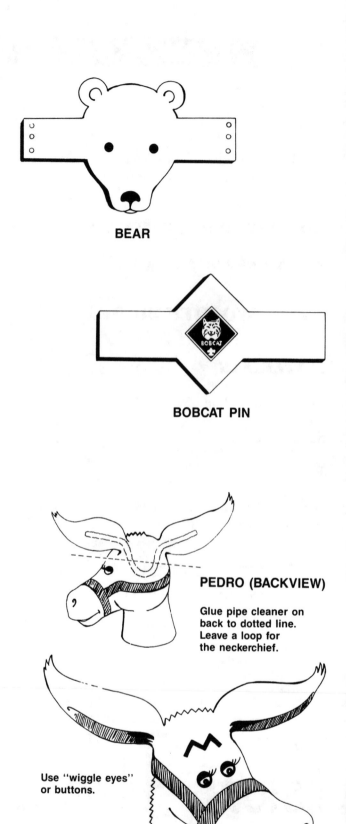

BEAR

BOBCAT PIN

BOBCAT

PEDRO (BACKVIEW)

Glue pipe cleaner on back to dotted line. Leave a loop for the neckerchief.

Use "wiggle eyes" or buttons.

***BOYS' LIFE* PEDRO**

HAT, SLIDE, OR NECKERCHIEF HOLDER

Use this holder to store your hat, slides, or neckerchief.

ADVANCEMENT POSSIBILITIES

Wolf Elective 3: Make It Yourself

Webelos Craftsman Activity Badge

MATERIALS

7" circle of ¾" pine board or plywood

2½" circle of ¾" pine board or plywood

10" length of 1" dowel rod

¼" pine board or plywood for wolf or bear head

Wood glue

Small nails

Paint, stain, or varnish, if desired

Sandpaper

Coping saw

Hammer

PROCEDURE

1. Cut out and sand 7" and 2½" circles for base and top.

2. Using a coping saw, cut out the wolf or bear heads, following the patterns shown. Sand the edges smooth.

3. Glue, then nail, 2½" circle to one end of the dowel.

4. Glue, then nail, 7" circle to the other end of the dowel to form the base.

5. Glue the head to the dowel.

6. Paint or stain, if you like.

7. Now you can put your neckerchief slides on the wolf or bear ears; the hat goes on top of the holder, and your neckerchief fits around the ears.

PATTERNS

13

DECORATIVE SLIDE HOLDER

Use the neckerchief slide holder to show off your slides and to decorate your room.

ADVANCEMENT POSSIBILITIES

Wolf Achievement 6: Start a Collection

Bear Elective 22: Collecting Things

Webelos Craftsman Activity Badge

MATERIALS

¼" pine board or plywood

Several nails

Coping saw

Sandpaper

Clean tuna or cat food can

4"–5" length of dowel

Plaster of paris powder

Photo of yourself

PROCEDURE

1. Draw a pattern from your own hand onto the pine board or plywood. Be sure to spread your fingers out.

2. Cut the pattern out with a coping saw. Sand the edges smooth.

3. Paint the hand as desired. Glue a picture of yourself in your Cub Scout uniform into the palm of the wooden hand.

4. Nail the completed hand onto the 4" or 5" dowel. Put several small nails into the end which will be covered with plaster.

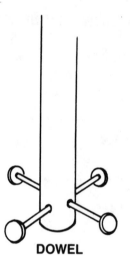

DOWEL

5. Fill the can ⅔ full of water and add plaster of paris powder until thick and creamy. When partially set, stand the dowel stick with hand upright in plaster and let harden completely.

6. Now you can put your neckerchief slides on the fingers. You can even drape your neckerchief over the thumb.

TRACK YOUR ADVANCEMENT WITH A
COUP STICK
(Pronounced: *Coo stick*)

Keep a personal record of your advancement using a coup stick.

There are a lot of different ways of making a coup stick. Here are two examples. Perhaps you can invent other coup sticks.

WEBELOS SCOUT COUP STICK

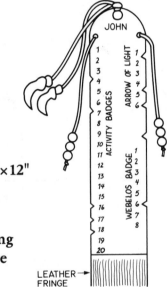

MATERIALS

¼" pine board, 1½" × 12"

Markers

Several pieces of thong and beads to decorate as you desire

PROCEDURE

1. Shape the piece of pine by sanding the edges.

2. Using a marker, number down the side of the piece of pine from 1 to 20 for activity badges, and down the opposite side from 1 to 8 for Webelos badge requirements and 1 to 6 for Arrow of Light requirements.

3. As you complete each activity badge or rank requirement, notch the edge with your pocketknife.

COUP STICK

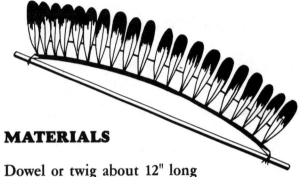

MATERIALS

Dowel or twig about 12" long

Feathers

Glue

18" leather thong or yarn

PROCEDURE

1. Cut two 2" pieces from thong.

2. Lay the end of the twig and the end of the long piece of thong on a short piece of the thong as shown.

3. Wrap and glue as shown.

4. As you pass each achievement, add a feather to the thong with thread.

Beads, bear claws, bells, and other items may be added to your coup stick to represent participation in day camp, Webelos overnighters, and other events.

BIKE RODEO ON A STRING

Improve your bike-riding skills and challenge a friend to a contest of riding skills.

ADVANCEMENT POSSIBILITY

Bear Achievement 14: Ride Right

MATERIALS

Two pieces of string, each at least 30' long

Four coffee cans, juice cans, or cans of similar size filled with rocks or dirt

Your bike

PROCEDURE

Tie a can to the end of each length of string. In all events, except the slalom, the rider loses one point when his bike wheel touches the string.

EVENTS

STRAIGHT RIDE

Lay the strings out parallel to each other 6″ apart. Ride from one end to the other between strings.

COASTING

Take your bike 10' back from where the string line begins. Pedal fast up to the strings then coast between them. The longest coast wins.

SLOW RACE

Spread the strings 3' apart. Pedal slowly without touching your feet to the ground or touching the strings. Have a friend time you with a wristwatch. The slowest ride time wins.

FIGURE 8

Line up the strings 9' apart and 18' long. Ride figure 8's inside the string lines without going outside open ends.

QUICK STOP

Ride up to one string from the side and brake to a stop 3″ from the string.

SLALOM

Make one long line of both strings with loops every 6′. Ride back and forth across the strings between the loops without touching them. If your bike wheel touches the loop, you lose.

ALWAYS RIDE SAFELY!

ESCAPE TURN

Ride up to one string from the side. When you are 1′ short of the string, turn left. Next time turn right.

EMERGENCY IDENT-A-CARD

Have an identification card and emergency phone money with you at all times.

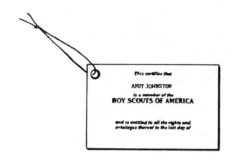

This certifies that

ANDY JOHNSTON

is a member of the
BOY SCOUTS OF AMERICA

and is entitled to all the rights and privileges thereof to the last day of

FRONT

MATERIALS

Piece of white paper the same size as your BSA membership card

BSA membership card

Hole puncher

Quarter

Leather thong

Self-stick clear plastic laminate or contact plastic

Pen

PROCEDURE

1. Cut the paper the same size as your BSA identification card.

2. Following the illustration, write your address, parent's name, phone number, medical information, and the name of your church or synagogue.

3. Glue on the quarter.

4. Seal the cards in the clear plastic, following the manufacturer's directions.

5. If desired, punch a hole in one corner of the plastic holder and thread leather thong through it to wear around your neck like a dog tag.

The plastic seal can be broken easily to reach the emergency phone money. After using the quarter, make new card and seal it.

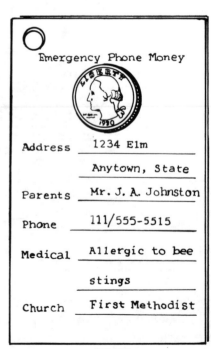

BACK

POCKETKNIFE HOLDER

The pocketknife holder provides a safe way to carry your pocketknife.

ADVANCEMENT POSSIBILITY

Webelos Craftsman Activity Badge

MATERIALS

Vinyl or leather

Rubber cement

Leather punch to make holes

Craftstrip lacing

PROCEDURE

1. Cut two pieces of vinyl or leather—the first the full size of the pattern shown, and the second just the bottom half, up to the dotted line. Cut two slits on bottom half, as illustrated. You may wish to create your own pattern to tool into the leather or put your initials on it.

2. If you wish to carry the holder on your belt, cut two slits marked by the dotted lines.

3. Lightly glue the bottom halves together (around sides and bottom), using rubber cement.

4. Punch holes an equal distance apart all around the sides and bottom.

5. Lace through the holes, starting at the top of one side and ending on the opposite side.

6. Your knife fits into the pocket and the top fits into the two slits to keep the holder closed.

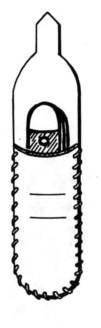

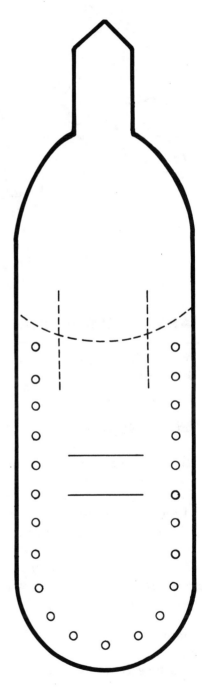

EMERGENCY SIGNAL

For safety purposes, keep an emergency road signal in your car.

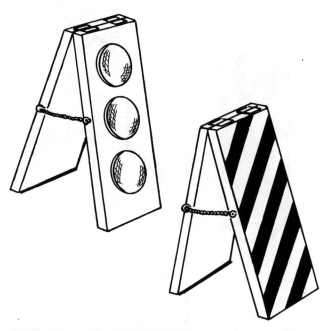

ADVANCEMENT POSSIBILITY

Wolf Achievement 5: Tools for Fixing and Building

MATERIALS

Two 1" hinges with screws

Two small screw-eyes

12" plumber's chain or wire

Reflector tape or glass reflectors

Screwdriver

Hammer

Two boards 4" x 24" x ¾"

Sandpaper

PROCEDURE

1. Cut the boards to right lengths and sand edges smooth.

2. Nail the reflectors to one side of each board, or apply reflector tape in several strips on each board.

3. Using a screwdriver, screw the hinges to the top of both boards.

4. Measure 8" from the bottom of each board and then screw in a screw-eye at that point. Attach the plumber's chain or wire between the eyes.

   If your car breaks down at night, place the emergency signal on the highway a reasonable distance in back of the car.

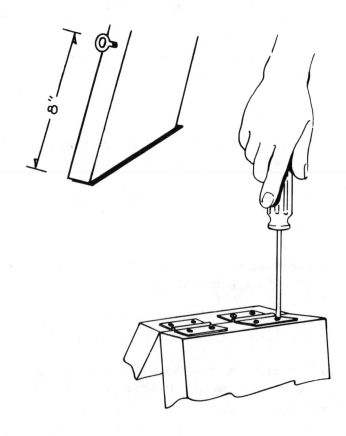

OWL MESSAGE HOLDER

Your mother, neighbor, or teacher might enjoy this handy gift.

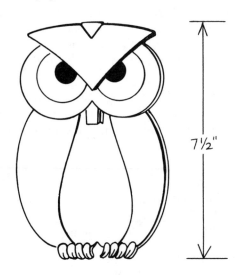

ADVANCEMENT POSSIBILITIES

Wolf Elective 3: Make It Yourself

Wolf Elective 9: Let's Have a Party

Webelos Craftsman Activity Badge

MATERIALS

¼" plywood

One spring-type clothespin

Hand drill with ⅛" bit

Several small nails

Hammer

Fine sandpaper

Paint in colors you choose

Screwdriver

PROCEDURE

1. Enlarge the head and body of an owl and transfer to a ¼" piece plywood as shown.

2. Cut out the piece with a coping saw and smooth with sandpaper. Paint as desired.

3. Separate the clothespin into two halves, making sure the spring stays on one half. Nail the half with the spring to the body of the owl as indicated by the dotted line.

4. Drill a small hole in the top of the body, through the clothespin. This will allow the holder to be hung on a wall.

5. Nail the remaining half of the clothespin to the back of the head piece, placing the top of the clothespin even with the top of the owl's head.

6. Use a screwdriver to lift the clothespin spring and reassemble the clothespin.

Now the clothespin forms the beak of the owl and you can use it to hold recipes or messages.

NOTE: The head and body may be glued to the clothespin instead of using nails. You don't have to take the clothespin apart to glue it.

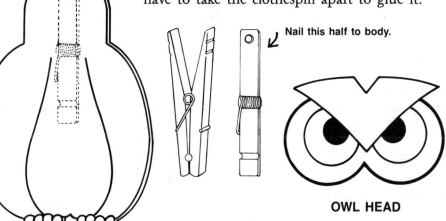

OWL BODY

Nail this half to body.

OWL HEAD

HURRICANE LAMP

Make a friendly light for evening activities in your yard.

ADVANCEMENT POSSIBILITY

Wolf Elective 3: Make It Yourself

MATERIALS

Saw

Candle

Sharp knife

One-half cup of flour

Hammer and nail

Broomstick or long stick of wood

Clean tuna or cat food can

Medium-size screw and screwdriver

Small jar that fits inside the can

PROCEDURE

1. Mix a half cup of flour with water to make a thick paste. Drop the ball of paste into the bottom of a small jar and set a candle in it. Allow the paste to dry thoroughly.

2. Saw off the top of a broomstick to make a flat surface. Then, with a sharp knife, whittle the other end of the stick to a point.

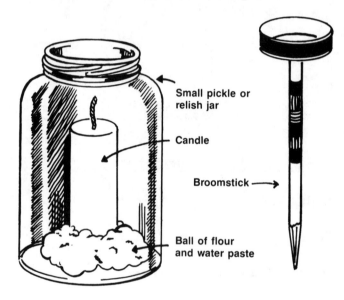

Small pickle or relish jar

Candle

Broomstick →

Ball of flour and water paste

3. With a hammer, pound down any rough edges along the top of the can.

4. Use a hammer and a nail to punch a hole in the bottom center of the can and then screw the can to the top of the broomstick.

5. Paint and decorate the lamp holder. You can paint a narrow band of color around the rim of the candle jar if you want the jar to match the holder.

6. Punch the holder into the ground and set the candle jar in the holder.

This easy-to-make hurricane lamp gives a friendly light for nighttime picnics and backyard gatherings.

TIN CAN LANTERN

Have a light for a patio table, decorate a room for a party, or give this lantern to someone special.

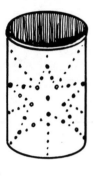

ADVANCEMENT POSSIBILITIES

Wolf Elective 3: Make It Yourself

Wolf Elective 9: Let's Have a Party

Webelos Craftsman Activity Badge

MATERIALS

Clean tin can, any size

Paper, pencil, and scissors

Several sizes of nails

Hammer

Small candle or votive candle

Funnel (optional)

Small glass jar that fits inside the can

PROCEDURE

1. Cut a piece of paper just big enough to fit around the can. Draw a design on the paper, then lay the paper aside.

2. Fill the can almost full of water and freeze solid.

3. Lay the can of ice on a towel and wrap the paper around the can. Tape it securely.

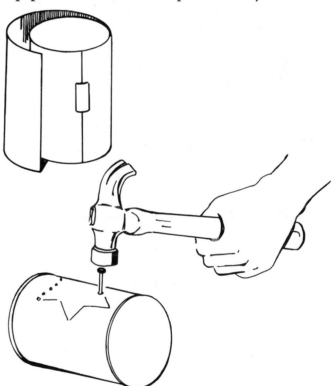

4. Now, hammer evenly spaced holes through the lines in your design using different sizes of nails.

5. Punch holes in the funnel if you want a lid for your lantern.

6. After the ice has melted, dry the can. Put a small candle in the glass jar and place the jar in the bottom of your lantern. Place the funnel upside down for a top.

CATAPULT

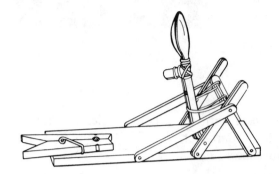

ADVANCEMENT POSSIBILITY

Webelos Engineer Activity Badge

MATERIALS

Eleven craft sticks

Piece of 1⅜" × ⅜" pine or pine lattice stock 8¼" long

Clothespin

15" length of strong twine

Plastic spoon, with only ¾" of handle left

Rubber band

Two small corks

Two 2" nails and a 1¾" nail

Two ½" pieces drinking straw

Six ½" wood screws

Hand drill

Glue

Knife

PROCEDURE

To make the catapult arm:

1. Glue two craft sticks together. Cut a ½" slot at one end for the handle of the plastic spoon. At the other end, drill a hole for one of the 2" nails.

2. Make two notches ½" apart (centered) in the bottom edge of the arm.

3. Cut a 1¼" piece of craft stick and glue it to the side of the arm at the slotted end. The top of the piece should be even with the bottom of the slot and it should extend down below the arm.

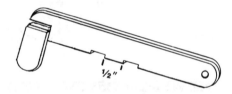

4. When the glue is dry, insert the spoon and wind the twine around the arm, spoon handle, and the extending piece of stick. Tie or glue the twine and trim off the excess.

To make the base and frame:

5. Use a 1⅜" × ⅜" piece of wood for the base. Drill a hole in each side of the base, 3" from the front edge and about ⅜" deep.

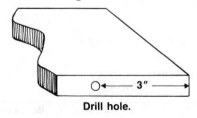

Drill hole.

6. Use masking tape or rubber bands to fasten four craft sticks into a stack, with all edges lined up. Drill holes through all four sticks as follows: a hole for a screw at one end, a nail hole 1″ from the screw hole, and another nail hole 2⅛″ from that one. After drilling, remove the tape or rubber bands. These four pieces are *uprights*.

7. Make another stack of four craft sticks and drill holes for screws at each end. Remove the tape or rubber bands and you have four diagonal supports.

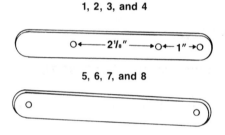

1, 2, 3, and 4

O← — 2⅛″ — →O←— 1″ —→O

5, 6, 7, and 8

Assemble the catapult as follows:

8. Put two uprights together and fasten them to one side of the base with a screw through the bottom holes of the uprights into the hole in the base. Do the same on the other side. The uprights should stand straight up from the base.

9. Attach diagonal supports to uprights by sliding a 2″ nail through the upper holes as shown. Push small cork onto the end of the nail to hold it.

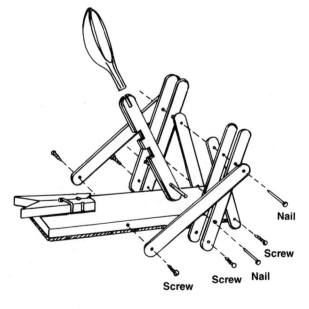

Nail

Screw

Screw Screw Nail

10. When the bottom ends of the diagonal sticks are positioned against the base, make pencil marks and drill holes in the base for the remaining wood screws. Securely screw the ends of the sticks to the base.

11. Loop a rubber band around the top nail and slip the bottom end of the catapult arm through the rubber-band loops. Insert the remaining 2″ nail through the upright sticks and the arm, placing the straw spacers on each side of the arm. Push the other small cork onto the end of the nail.

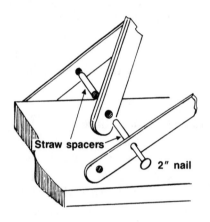

Straw spacers

2″ nail

12. Pull down the catapult arm and mark where the extended stick touches the base. Place the jaw of the clothespin on this mark and fasten the clothespin to the base with the 1¾″ nail.

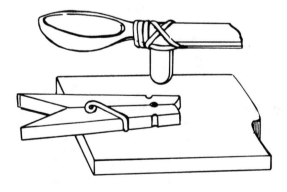

Now arm your catapult with small foil balls and fire away!

SAFETY FIRST! Never fire your catapult toward any person or animal. Use only foil balls as ammunition.

THE *ALMOST* PERPETUAL MOTION MACHINE

Two forces of nature—gravity and centrifugal force—team up to power this interesting mechanical movement. Set the machine on the edge of a table with the weight hanging over the side. Wind it up by rotating the boom clockwise until the cord is wrapped around the shaft. Release the boom, and your machine will go to work until it uses up all the string on the shaft.

For centuries, people have been trying to invent a perpetual motion machine. This model comes close to it in theory. In fact, if you could wrap a mile or more of string on the shaft and hang the weight over the edge of the Grand Canyon, it would work for days and days without requiring any attention—or until the parts wore out. That's why we call it a perpetual motion machine—well, almost!

ADVANCEMENT POSSIBILITY

Webelos Engineer Activity Badge

MATERIALS

Two 8" lengths of pine lattice stock ¼" × 1⅜"

Three 3½" lengths of pine lattice stock ¼" × 1⅜"

Screw-top baby food jar (or other small jar) with iron nuts or washers added so that it weighs 6–8 ounces

Two 7" lengths of ⅛" wood dowel

9½" length of clotheshanger wire

Two large machine bolt nuts

Long length of stout cord or nylon thread

Two small corks

Pliers

Glue

Hand drill

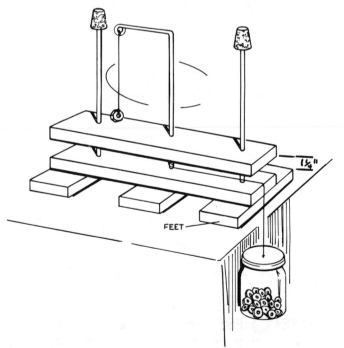

PROCEDURE

1. Tape the two long pieces of lattice stock together and be sure they line up perfectly. Drill three ⅛" holes in the long pieces of lattice stock.

2. Glue the three "feet" (the 3½" lengths) under the lower piece after the holes are drilled.

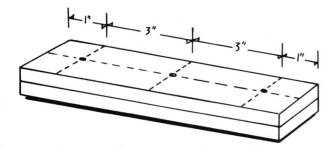

3. Push the dowels into the outermost holes of the frame, separating the top and bottom pieces by 1¼". Force corks onto the top ends of the dowels.

4. Form the shaft and boom by using pliers to make a right angle bend in the clotheshanger wire 6" from one end. Complete the boom by bending the end of the short section into a small circle.

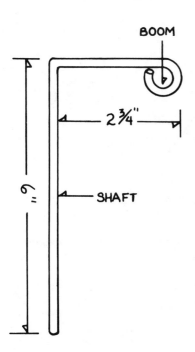

5. Tie one machine nut to a length of cord and tie the other end of the cord to the boom. The nut should just clear the top of the upper frame piece.

6. Insert the shaft into the center holes of the frame, then attach another cord to the shaft just below the top frame piece, using a timber hitch knot. (Apply a drop of glue or model cement to secure knot to shaft.)

7. Slip the other end of cord through a tiny hole in the bottle cap and tie the second nut at this end to anchor cord in cap. Screw cap back onto the filled bottle.

OPERATION

1. Place the machine on a table or other flat surface with the baby food jar hanging over the edge.

2. Turn the boom to wind the long cord around the shaft until the jar is as high as it will go.

3. Release the jar and watch the perpetual motion—almost!

A CLIMBING BEAR

Make this for a friend, children's home, church school, day care center, or hospital pediatrics ward.

ADVANCEMENT POSSIBILITIES

Wolf Elective 3: Make It Yourself

Wolf Elective 9: Let's Have a Party

Webelos Craftsman Activity Badge

MATERIALS

Three large wooden beads

Four upholstery nails or ⅝" box nails

Two red thumbtacks (for noses)

Black felt-tip pen to draw mouth

9' of cotton or nylon cord

Coping saw

Sandpaper

One piece hardwood or pinewood, ¾" × 5" × 5¾"

One hanging bar of pinewood, ¾" × ¾" × 6¾"

Hand drill with ⅜" bit

Paint or stain, if desired

PROCEDURE

1. Enlarge pattern and transfer onto large piece of hardwood or pinewood.

2. Cut out with coping saw. Then drill holes through arms at the exact angle shown by the dotted lines. Sand until smooth.

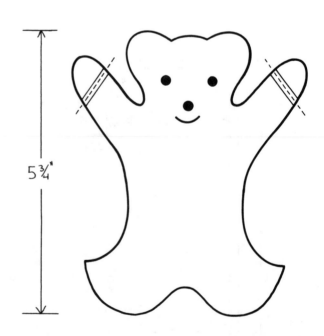

5¾"

28

3. Stain or paint as desired. Let it dry before going to next step.

4. Use nails and thumbtacks to make eyes and noses on both sides. Draw mouth lines with felt-tip pen.

5. Drill holes in bar as indicated in this drawing.

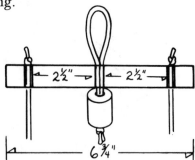

6. Cut two 50" long pieces of cord and thread them through the bar, bear, and beads. Then knot the ends. Using remaining cord as the center for the support, passing it through the bar and bead.

7. Now hang the cord loop on a hook in the wall or ceiling and pull alternately on the cord ends to make the bear climb. Be sure to pull straight down. When he reaches the top, release both cords and the bear will slide to the bottom again.

WANT TO TRY ANOTHER CLIMBER?

Using the same basic pattern, change the shape of the ears and head to make another animal. Or try making a "climbing clown," complete with funny hat and polka-dot suit, or even a Martian with pointed ears and green pipe-cleaner antennae.

BOX PUZZLES

Test your own skills or give this puzzle to a friend, family member, or someone who is sick in bed and needs some entertainment.

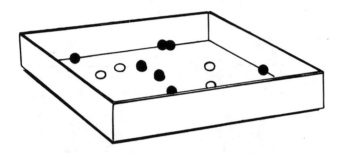

ADVANCEMENT POSSIBILITIES

Wolf Achievement 10: Family Fun

Wolf Elective 9: Let's Have a Party

MATERIALS

Any size greeting card box with clear acetate cover

Piece of lightweight cardboard same size as box

Construction paper or contact-type vinyl plastic sheeting

Buttons, cake decoration silvers, or ball bearings

Heavy scissors

Awl

PROCEDURE

1. Cut your box sides down so that they are ¾" high. Draw lines around box, making sure they meet in all corners. Use heavy scissors or tin snips to cut.

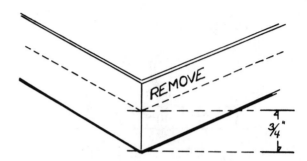

2. Decide on your puzzle "theme" or idea and draw it onto the lightweight cardboard. Punch out the holes for the cake silvers or ball bearings with the awl (don't make the holes too large). "Lakes," "rivers," and the like can be cut with scissors.

3. Cover your design with construction paper and glue it down or cover it with contact vinyl. Be sure to transfer the holes, also.

4. Now, add the appropriate number of markers and tape the lid on top of the puzzle.

TO PLAY: Try to get all the balls into the holes; or move them from one point to another, avoiding hazards along the way. Happy puzzling!

TRIM THE TREE

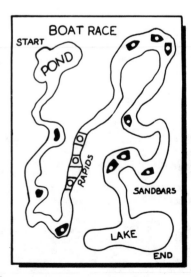

BOAT RACE

PAULSON'S PIPER

Learn new woodworking skills while making this toy.

ADVANCEMENT POSSIBILITIES

Webelos Craftsman Activity Badge

Wolf Elective 3: Make It Yourself

MATERIALS

¾" pine board larger than bird pattern

18" of ¼" dowel rod

Coathanger

Sandpaper

Coping saw

Paint in desired colors

6"×6" pine board for base

Hand drill with ¼" bit

Finishing nail

PROCEDURE

1. Enlarge the pattern and transfer onto pine board. Cut out with a coping saw and sand the edges smooth. (See "How to Enlarge a Pattern" on page 8.)

2. Paint the bird in desired colors.

3. Straighten a coathanger and make several wraps around the dowel as shown. Make a loop close to the wrapped wire (see illustration).

4. Make a small hole in the bird with a finishing nail. Insert the wire into the bird and place on the dowel.

5. Use a hand drill to make a hole in the center of the base.

6. Insert into the base as shown.

Now, flip the tail and watch your bird go into action.

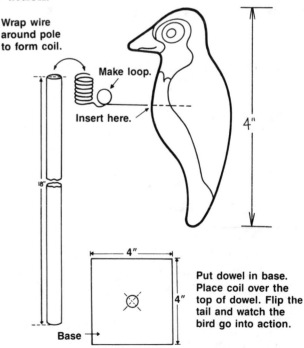

Wrap wire around pole to form coil.

Make loop.

Insert here.

4"

18"

Base

4"

4"

Put dowel in base. Place coil over the top of dowel. Flip the tail and watch the bird go into action.

RACE CARS

Have fun while challenging a friend to a contest.

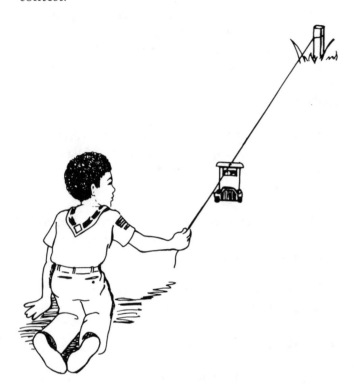

ADVANCEMENT POSSIBILITY

Webelos Craftsman Activity Badge

MATERIALS

Board — particle board, pine paneling scrap, or plywood

Coping saw or jigsaw

Hand drill

15' to 20' heavy cord or twine

Sandpaper

Paint or stain as desired

PROCEDURE

1. Enlarge the patterns in this book, following the directions for enlarging on page 8.

2. Cut from your selected board, using a coping saw or jigsaw. Sand the edges smooth.

3. Drill a hole slightly larger than the cord. Center it about 1″ from the top of the car.

4. Paint your cars as you wish. You may put your name on the license plate.

TO PLAY: Thread the cord through the hole and fasten one end to a sturdy object (one that won't move). Now, alternately tighten and relax the cord and your car will move *toward* you. Have a race with a friend.

NOTE: Instead of race cars, draw a locomotive (old or modern), a dog and a cat, a cat and a mouse, or other "racers."

CUB SCOUT'S
NAME

CUB SCOUT'S
NAME OR
DEN NUMBER

CUB SCOUT'S NAME

CUB SCOUT'S
NAME OR
DEN NUMBER

PLAY TIC-TAC-TOE

Play this game with friends or family members.

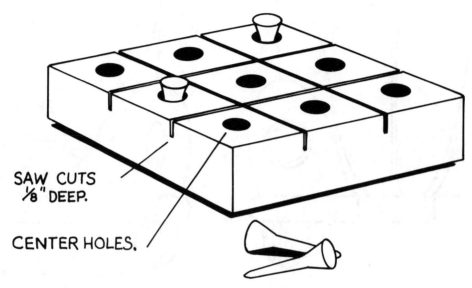

SAW CUTS
⅛" DEEP.

CENTER HOLES.

ADVANCEMENT POSSIBILITY

Webelos Craftsman Activity Badge

MATERIALS

Hand drill with ³⁄₁₆ " bit

Saw

Sandpaper

10 golf tees in 2 colors

Block of wood 4" × 4" × 1" thick

PROCEDURE

1. Cut a block of wood. Sand all edges until smooth.

2. Mark each side into thirds with a pencil. Draw lines—this will make nine equal-size squares.

3. Saw along each line, making cuts about ⅛" deep. You may also wish to paint these lines.

4. Use hand drill with ³⁄₁₆" bit to drill nine holes, each centered in one of the nine squares, almost to the bottom of block.

TO PLAY: Use 10 golf tees—5 of each of 2 colors—and play like regular tic-tac-toe.

NOTE: Instead of sawing lines, you can make them with felt-tip markers or a woodburning pen.

POP-UT

Play this game with a friend.

MATERIALS

3 feathers about 10" long

Old sock

Rubber band

3" diameter cardboard circle

Paper punch

Masking tape

Old rags or used pantyhose (for stuffing)

PROCEDURE

1. Punch three holes in the cardboard circle. Insert feathers, bend over their points and tape in place.

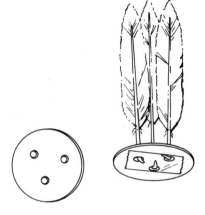

2. Cut off about 5" from toe of sock and stuff with old rags or pantyhose.

3. Insert the cardboard and feather disk into the top of the stuffed sock. Fasten with a rubber band.

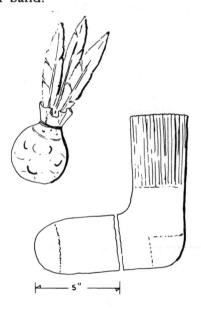

TO PLAY: Hit the pop-ut with the palm of your hand (back and forth) and try to keep it from hitting the ground.

SCOOP GAME

Play catch with a friend or a family member

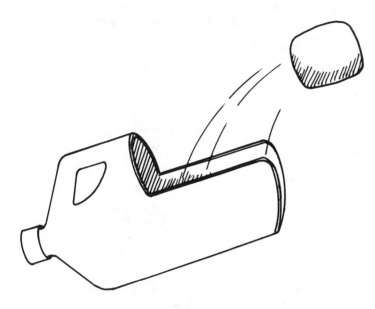

MATERIALS

Plastic milk or bleach bottle

Scissors

4" × 8" piece of fabric (old jeans work well)

Rice or beans (dried)

Needle and thread

PROCEDURE

1. Wash bottle thoroughly.

2. Cut bottom and part of one side from bottle as indicated in the drawing. Your "scooper" is complete. Make a second one for your friend.

3. Fold fabric in half, right sides in, forming a 4" × 4" square. Sew almost around the square. Turn right side out. Fill with dried beans or rice.

4. Sew the opening closed with slip stitch.

5. Place beanbag in "scooper" and toss it underhanded to your friend. Practice catching and throwing the beanbag from the "scooper." You can also use a rubber ball, sponge ball, or foil ball to play catch.

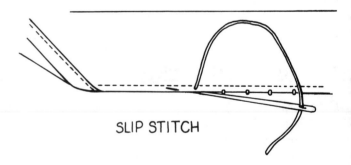

SLIP STITCH

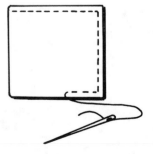

MAKE A CATAPULT TO LAUNCH A PARACHUTE

Challenge a friend to a contest for distance or height.

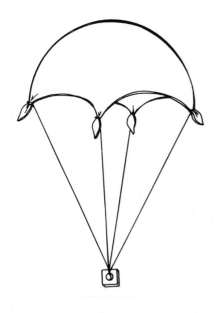

MATERIALS

Nail

Hammer

Small screw

Screwdriver

String or heavy thread

Small nut or washer

Small mustard or pickle jar lid

Lightweight cloth about 10" to 12" square

Stick of light wood about 18" × 2"

PROCEDURE

To make the catapult:

1. Using a hammer and a nail, punch a hole in the center of a small jar lid. Fasten the lid to the stick of wood with a small screw.

2. If the screw protrudes through the back side of the stick of wood, slip two or three nuts between the lid and the wood to take up the extra length. Remember, safety first!

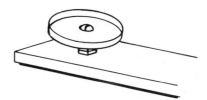

To make the parachute:

3. Tie a piece of 12" string tightly to each corner of a cleansing tissue or lightweight cloth. Then hold the corners of the parachute even, slip the strings through a nut or washer, and tie with a square knot.

4. Test the parachute by tossing it into the air. If it sails to the ground too fast, the nut is too heavy.

To launch the parachute:

5. Mark a pencil line across the catapult 6″ from the end opposite the jar lid. This is the lever point.

6. Fold the parachute and wrap the strings loosely around it. Then place the parachute in the jar lid.

7. Use left hand to hold catapult on top of fence or porch railing. Strike end of board with right fist.

8. The parachute will open as it is projected into the air.

BOOMERANG!

This boomerang is a simple one, but it will work exactly like the boomerangs used by natives in Australia, South America, and India. You can make it whirl across the room and return to the spot from which you threw it.

ADVANCEMENT POSSIBILITY

Wolf Elective 9: Let's Have a Party

MATERIALS

Scissors

Pencil

Cardboard

Carbon paper

Book

PROCEDURE

1. Trace the boomerang pattern on a piece of stiff cardboard and cut it out.

2. Lay the boomerang on a book or magazine with one prong extending over the side of the book.

3. Tip the front of the book up a little and hit the prong of the boomerang with a quick forward stroke of a pencil.

If you hit it correctly, the boomerang will whirl out across the room and return to the spot where you are standing.

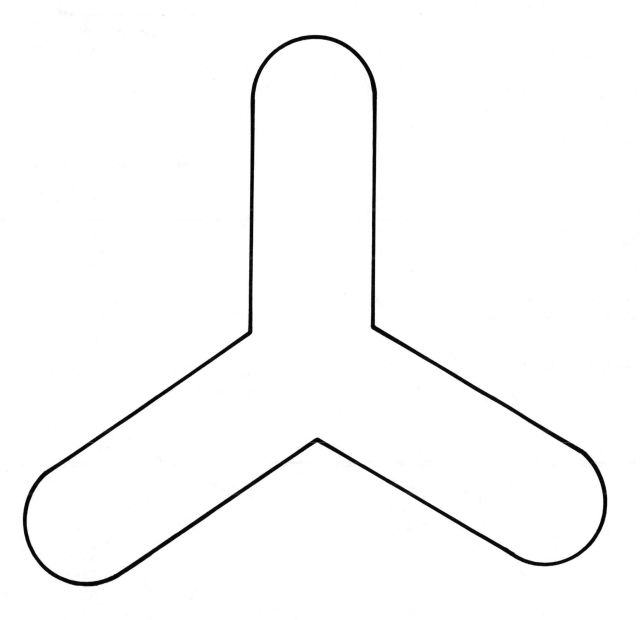

HIGH-FLYING KITE

See how high you can make it go, then challenge a friend to a contest.

ADVANCEMENT POSSIBILITY

Wolf Elective 5: Sparetime Fun

MATERIALS

Two kite sticks (1/8" dowel sticks or long narrow flat sticks)

Ball of strong string

Sheet of strong, lightweight paper, 36"×34" (wrapping paper makes colorful kites)

Paper reinforcers

Coping saw or hobby knife

Scissors

Pencil

Ruler

White glue, paste, or glue stick

PROCEDURE

1. Cut the two kite sticks to size, then notch ends.

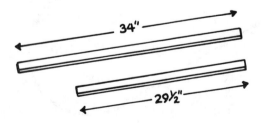

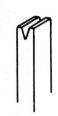

USE COPING SAW TO NOTCH ENDS OF STICKS OR USE SINGLE-EDGE RAZOR BLADE. IF YOU USE A RAZOR BLADE, CUT TOWARDS CENTER TO AVOID SPLITTING STICKS.

CUT NOTCHES PARALLEL TO WIDE SIDE OF STICK.

2. Tie the two sticks together.

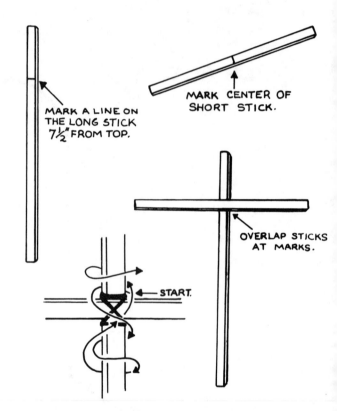

MARK A LINE ON THE LONG STICK 7½" FROM TOP.

MARK CENTER OF SHORT STICK.

OVERLAP STICKS AT MARKS.

START.

3. String outer edge of the kite frame, slipping string through notches at ends of sticks, then tie.

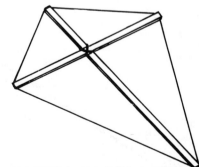

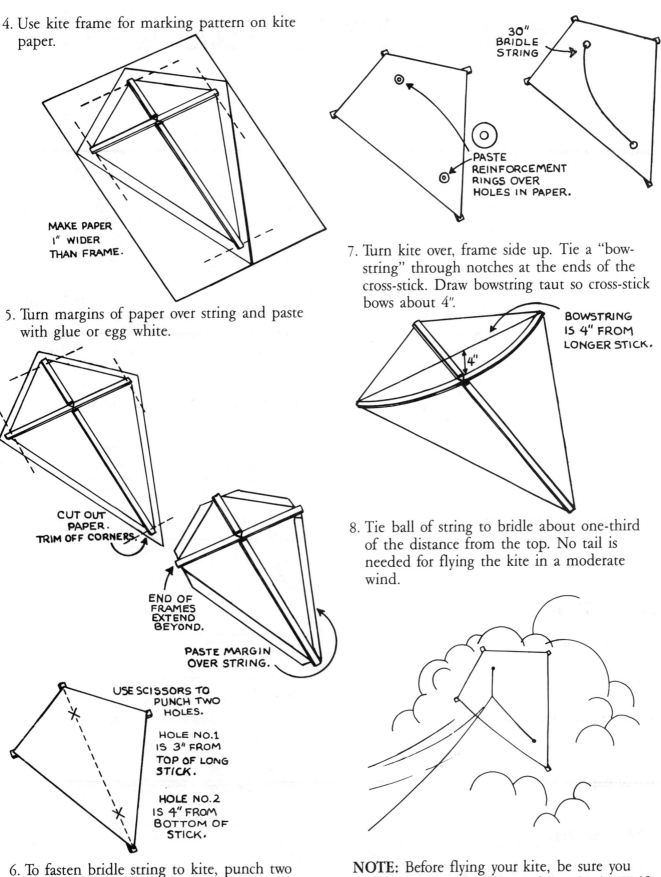

4. Use kite frame for marking pattern on kite paper.

MAKE PAPER 1" WIDER THAN FRAME.

5. Turn margins of paper over string and paste with glue or egg white.

CUT OUT PAPER. TRIM OFF CORNERS.

END OF FRAMES EXTEND BEYOND.

PASTE MARGIN OVER STRING.

USE SCISSORS TO PUNCH TWO HOLES.

HOLE NO.1 IS 3" FROM TOP OF LONG STICK.

HOLE NO.2 IS 4" FROM BOTTOM OF STICK.

6. To fasten bridle string to kite, punch two holes in the paper and tie a 30" string to the longer stick.

30" BRIDLE STRING

PASTE REINFORCEMENT RINGS OVER HOLES IN PAPER.

7. Turn kite over, frame side up. Tie a "bowstring" through notches at the ends of the cross-stick. Draw bowstring taut so cross-stick bows about 4".

BOWSTRING IS 4" FROM LONGER STICK.

4"

8. Tie ball of string to bridle about one-third of the distance from the top. No tail is needed for flying the kite in a moderate wind.

NOTE: Before flying your kite, be sure you understand the kite-flying safety rules in Wolf elective 6.

FLY A MINIATURE KITE

See how high a little kite can fly.

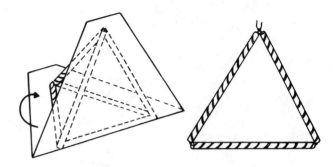

2. Make a pyramid, adding the other 3 straws.

3. Lay completed pyramid on the tissue paper. Cut one piece of tissue paper 2" larger on all sides than *two* sides of the pyramid frame.

4. Fold edges over frame, cutting it to fit. Glue down.

ADVANCEMENT POSSIBILITY

Wolf Elective 5: Sparetime Fun

MATERIALS

Six soda straws

Glue

Kite string

Scissors

Tissue paper

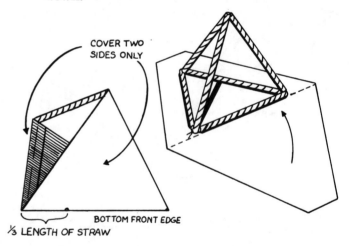

COVER TWO SIDES ONLY

BOTTOM FRONT EDGE

⅓ LENGTH OF STRAW

5. Measure one-third of the distance from front edge of kite down the covered side. Attach 12" length of kite string.

6. Attach rest of kite string at the top of the tail of the kite. Tie two strings together.

7. Attach several 2" wide strips of tissue paper at the bottom front edge of the kite for a tail.

NOTE: This kite will fly easily in even light winds!

PROCEDURE

1. Insert kite string through three straws to make a triangle. Tie the string securely and cut off excess.

BUTTON BUTTON

Challenge a parent or friend to this game. Give one to a sick-in-bed friend as a gift.

ADVANCEMENT POSSIBILITY

Wolf Elective 9: Let's Have a Party

MATERIALS

Five buttons

Tracing paper

Cardboard

Glue

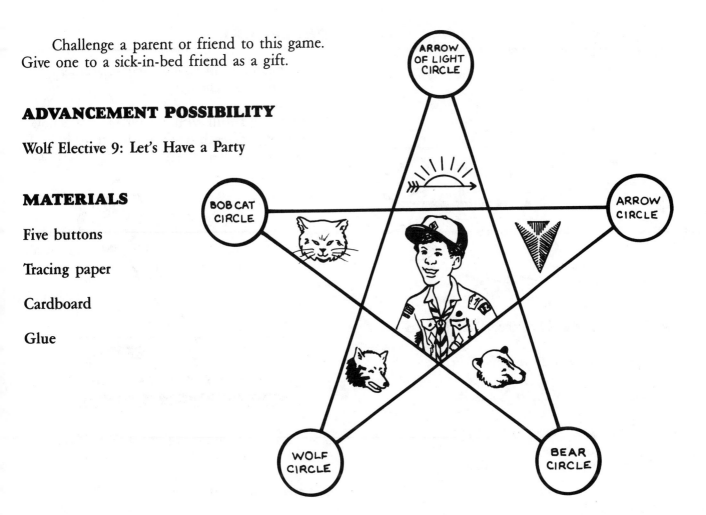

PROCEDURE

Trace the pattern and mount it on cardboard with glue.

TO PLAY: Fill all the circles on the points of the star with buttons.

1. Place a button in any circle and slide it across the star, following one of the straight lines, to another open circle.

2. After a button has been moved across the star, it cannot be moved again.

3. No more than one button can occupy a circle.

4. Move the second, third, and fourth buttons, one by one, in the same manner as you did the first.

5. The fifth button is placed directly in the only remaining open circle.

SOLUTION

If your first button was moved from the Arrow of Light circle to the Bear circle, then your second button must be moved to fill the Arrow of Light circle, etc. The trick is to slide the button to the circle that was last used as a starting point.

GO·ZIN·TA

Play this game with family or friends, or give it to someone special.

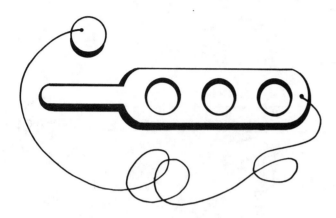

ADVANCEMENT POSSIBILITIES

Wolf Achievement 10: Family Fun

Wolf Elective 3: Make It Yourself

Wolf Elective 9: Let's Have a Party

Webelos Craftsman Activity Badge

MATERIALS

½" board 5"×24"

Old tennis ball or other rubber ball

4' length of strong cord

Sandpaper

Coping saw

Keyhole saw

Hand drill

PROCEDURE

1. Cut board. Sand edges. Draw placement of holes with a pencil.

2. Use a hand drill with ½" bit to drill a hole near edge of each opening. Insert keyhole saw and saw out holes.

3. Drill a ¹⁄₁₆" hole at end of Go-Zin-Ta and insert strong cord. Knot underneath.

4. Fasten ball at other end of 4' cord.

TO PLAY: Toss ball into the air and catch it in one of the holes. Take turns playing with family members or friends. You may wish to give each hole a different point value, such as 5 for each of the end holes and 10 for the middle hole. Add up score to find the winner.

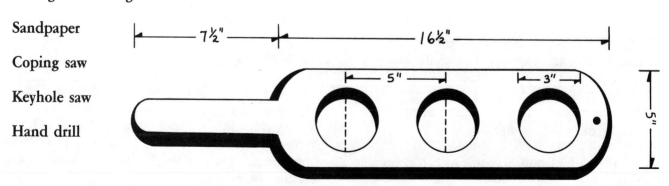

GAMES

Here are some game ideas to play with friends or family members.

ON TARGET

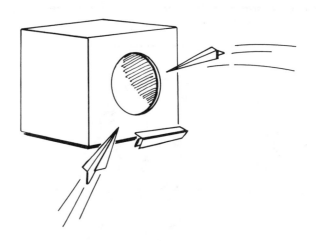

Cut a hole in the bottom of a cardboard carton as shown. Each player makes three paper airplanes of his own design. In turn, each player tosses his planes at the hole from 10' away. Score a point for every plane sailing through the hole. Make it more difficult or easier by varying the distance the plane is tossed.

NEST THE CANS

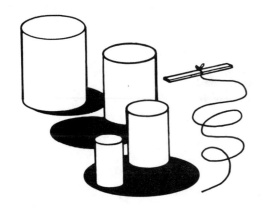

You'll need four empty cans of different sizes, a craft stick (with the ends cut square), and string. The cans must fit one inside the other easily.

Tie the string to the craft stick. Player holds the string, lowering stick into can, and when the stick has become wedged inside, he lifts the can and places it in the next largest one. Time how long it takes each player to nest all the cans. This is harder than it looks!

WINDSTORM

Play Windstorm with teams. An equal number of players take places at opposite sides of a table. Each player kneels so that his face is at tabletop level. A table tennis ball is placed at the center of the table. Players try to blow the ball off the opposite side. Touching the ball is *not* allowed. This is a fast and funny game.

BEANBAG TOSSING GAMES

Make beanbags (old jeans, vinyl, or socks are good fabric choices). Have fun tossing them at one of these targets. Be sure to throw them *underhanded*.

Use construction paper for hat and face.

SINGING SAM

SNOWMAN

MASKS

Wear one of these masks for skits at pack meetings or in school.

ADVANCEMENT POSSIBILITIES

Wolf Elective 2: Be an Actor

Bear Elective 10: Masks

MATERIALS

Brown paper bag

1-gal. plastic milk jug

Colored construction paper

Scissors

Glue

Broom straws

Soda straws

3-gal. ice-cream carton

Clean 1-gal. plastic bleach bottle

Scraps of felt

Yarn

PAPER-BAG MASK

Use soda straws for hair, construction paper for facial features, broom straws for whiskers, yarn for hair and mustaches. Use real or paper feathers where desired.

MILK-JUG MASK

A one-gallon plastic milk jug will make two masks. Cut along dotted line as indicated in the drawing.

The section with the handle can be used either side up, depending on the shape of the face you desire.

CUT ALONG THIS LINE

CUT OFF

HANDLE

MILK-JUG MASKS

PLASTIC BLEACH-BOTTLE MASK

Clean your bleach bottle thoroughly before beginning your mask.

Remove the bottom of the bleach bottle and cut the remaining part to the shape you desire. Cut from top to bottom along a straight line.

Attach strings through holes in the back to tie around your head.

ICE-CREAM CARTON MASK

This mask is made by turning the carton bottom-side up and creating the face you desire. Use scissors to cut out eyes and mouth. Add features with soda straws, broom straws, foil, corks, yarn, or whatever you can find that will do the job for you. This mask may be painted or covered with aluminum foil.

STRING ART

Use this project to decorate your room or give it to a friend, family member, or teacher.

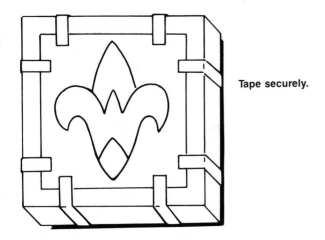

Tape securely.

ADVANCEMENT POSSIBILITY

Wolf Elective 3: Make It Yourself

MATERIALS

Board (pinewood, plywood, or particle board)

Yarn or crochet thread

Small headless nails (¾" nails or brads)

Design of your choice (original or from a book)

Hammer

Long-nosed pliers

Saw

Glue

Sandpaper

PROCEDURE

1. Cut board to a size several inches larger than your own design. Sand the edges.

2. If you wish, stain, paint, or cover your board with fabric (cut about 3" longer and wider than board—and nail, staple, or glue onto the back.)

3. Carefully tape your design over your board.

4. Hammer the nails (brads) about halfway into the board. A pair of tweezers or long-nosed pliers will help to hold the nails. Space nails about ½" apart. Carefully lift off the paper pattern.

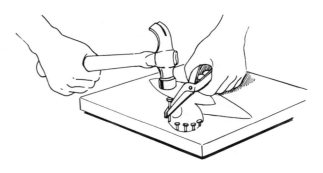

5. Attach yarn (for large patterns) or crochet thread (for smaller patterns) to one nail and wrap around the rest of the nails in sequence. It often looks nicer to have two or more layers of yarn or thread. (HINT: If you do not have enough string to finish a section, tie a knot at a nail, rather than between nails.)

6. When completed, a dab of white glue applied to knots will prevent them from coming loose.

7. Now attach a hanger on the back and display it in your room for all to admire.

Here is a pattern for a Webelos Scout
emblem. Coloring books and dot-to-dot books
are good sources for ideas.

WEBELOS SCOUT EMBLEM PLAQUE

Use a 10″×10″ board. You will need
42 brads, and yellow and blue crochet thread.
Begin at number 1 with blue thread. Follow
numbers 1-3-4-5-9-7-8 and back to number 1.
Repeat at least once. With yellow, follow numbers 1-2-3 and 3-2-1. Tie off. Start with yellow
at number 7 and follow numbers 7-6-5 and
5-6-7 and tie off. Look at a Webelos badge for
help.

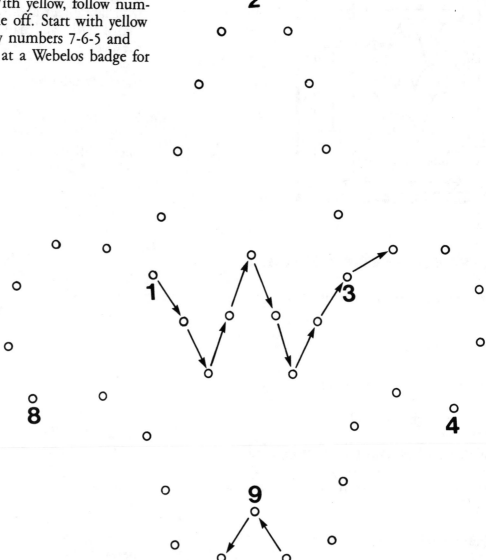

CRAYON BATIK

Create your own one-of-a-kind T-shirts, wall-hangings, patches, place mats, pictures, and the like.

MATERIALS

Cloth of lightweight and absorbent material or a T-shirt

Wax crayons—colors of your choice

Absorbent paper (paper towel, for instance)

Waxed paper

Iron and ironing board

PROCEDURE

Before beginning, be sure that you have an adult nearby to help with the ironing phase of this project.

1. Select your fabric or T-shirt and draw your design on it, using the wax crayons. Pile up the color somewhat by using pressure and going over the design more than once. Work the color into the cloth well.

2. Remove all the loose specks of crayon from the material or they will leave spots in the finished piece.

3. Place your material or T-shirt between two pieces of waxed paper. (If you use a T-shirt, place the absorbent paper and waxed paper inside the shirt—between the fabric layers.)

4. *With the help of an adult,* press your item with a hot iron. This will melt the crayon into the fabric, setting your design into the material.

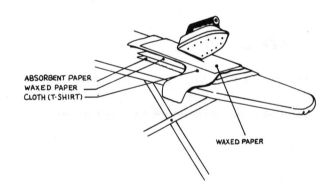

ABSORBENT PAPER
WAXED PAPER
CLOTH (T-SHIRT)

WAXED PAPER

5. Now you can frame your completed "batik" as a picture, hem it for a wall-hanging, put it on and show off your one-of-a-kind T-shirt, or use it as a costume for a skit!

NOTE: Your fabric or T-shirt can be washed in warm or cool water. If you use bleach your design will fade after a few launderings, but you can redo it.

A SPINNING COLOR WHEEL

This is a good gift for a sick friend who must stay in bed.

ADVANCEMENT POSSIBILITY

Wolf Elective 9: Let's Have a Party

MATERIALS

Two pieces of string about 28" long

Large needle, awl, or ice pick for punch

Scissors

Crayons or paints

Piece of cardboard

Two large buttons or spools

TO MAKE THE WHEEL

1. Cut out a heavy cardboard wheel the size of the wheels shown on page 53.

2. Color or paint the two sides of the wheel, using colors and design indicated.

3. At each point marked **X** on one side of the color wheel, punch a pin hole with a large needle or ice pick.

4. Thread pieces of string through each of the holes.

5. Thread the string ends through large buttons or spools (for handles) and tie.

TO OPERATE THE WHEEL

6. Gripping the color wheel by the handles, whirl the wheel around and around until the string is well twisted.

7. Now pull out slowly on the handles so that the wheel begins to whirl as the string untwists.

8. When the wheel has started to spin rapidly, let the strings hang slightly loose. The wheel will continue to spin until it winds the string in the opposite direction. Now you are ready to pull out slowly on the handles again, etc.

NOTE: A similar toy can be made using a large two-hole button instead of the color wheel. It works in the same way.

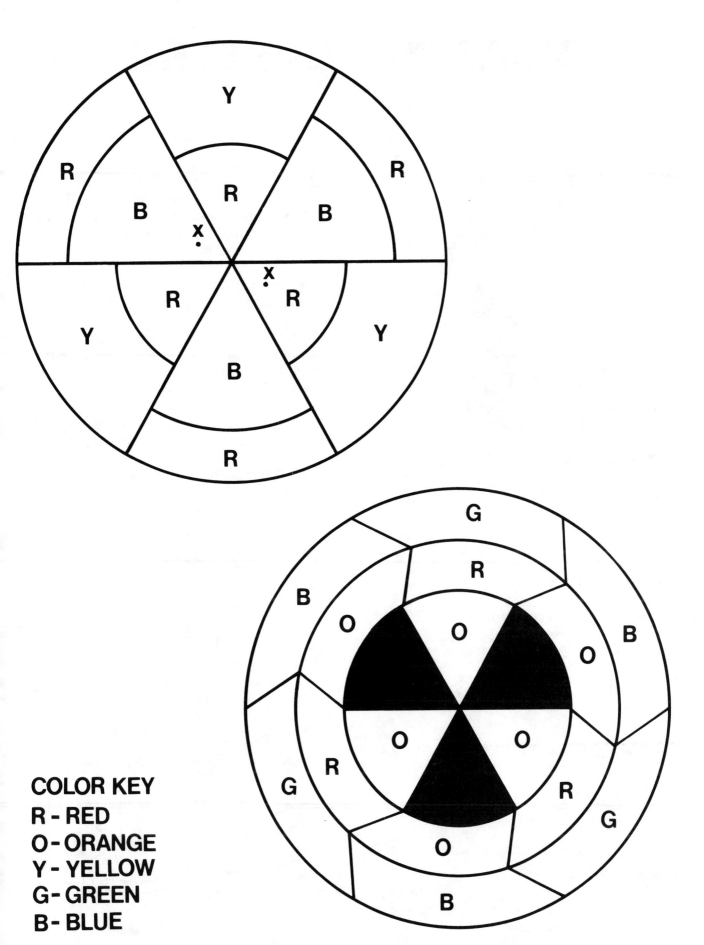

COLOR KEY
R - RED
O - ORANGE
Y - YELLOW
G - GREEN
B - BLUE

PLASTER CARVING

Develop your knife-handling skills and make something for your room.

ADVANCEMENT POSSIBILITY

Bear Achievement 19: Shavings and Chips

MATERIALS

1-qt. milk carton (clean)

Vermiculite (garden supply stores)

Plaster of paris

Pocketknife

Sandpaper

Tempera paint

Clear lacquer

Felt scraps, if desired

PROCEDURE

1. Measure equal amounts of vermiculite and plaster of paris in a can.

2. Add this mixture to water, mixing until creamy and fairly thick. Don't stir too much or you will get air in the mixture. (TIP: Measure the amount of water needed to fill your mold [milk carton], then add the vermiculite/plaster mix.)

3. Fill the milk carton with mixture and let it stand until it gets hard. Tear off the carton.

4. Using your pocketknife, carve your animal or other figure. Smooth with sandpaper. Paint with tempera paint and spray with clear lacquer.

5. If you want to add details, such as ears and eyes, glue felt pieces onto your sculpture.

NOTE: You may wish to use pint or even half-pint cartons.

BETSY ROSS STAR

Use these stars as table decorations, decorations on gift packages, or as place cards.

ADVANCEMENT POSSIBILITY

Wolf Elective 9: Let's Have a Party

MATERIALS

Scissors

4" square of very thin paper

PROCEDURE

1. Fold a 4" square of very thin paper in half and lay it on the table with the folded edge toward you.

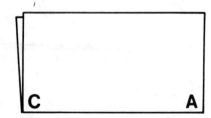

2. Lift corner A and fold it to touch the left-hand edge of the paper about one third the distance from the top to the bottom.

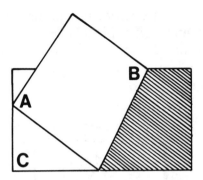

3. Lift corner B and fold it to touch corner A. Crease the folds with your fingernail to make the paper lie flat.

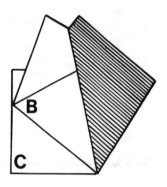

4. Lift corner C and fold it over the other folds of paper. Crease the fold with your fingernail.

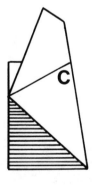
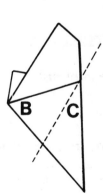

5. With your scissors, make one snip across the folded paper as shown by the dotted line.

6. Now, unfold the small triangle and you'll find a five-pointed Betsy Ross star as shown.

SPATTER PRINTING

Make a collection of leaf prints, or use this project to make gifts, birthday cards, or other greeting cards. Mount and hang it on the wall to decorate your room, or use it to make party decorations.

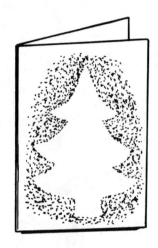

ADVANCEMENT POSSIBILITIES

Wolf Elective 9: Let's Have a Party

Wolf Achievement 6: Start a Collection

MATERIALS

Old toothbrush

Scissors

12" square piece of wire screen

Heavy paper for stencils or patterns

Better paper for final prints

Thinned water colors or poster paint

Containers for paint

Four 11¼" lengths of 1"×2" board

Eight 1½" nails

Tacks or small nails

Hammer

PROCEDURE

1. Lay leaf, a paper stencil, or other object to be printed on a sheet of paper.

2. Hold screen directly over cutout design, about 4 inches away from it. Then dip brush into thinned paint and shake off excess paint. Rub brush over screen, spattering tiny drops of color around and on your cutout or leaf. Practice on scrap paper first.

3. Remove cutout from paper, being careful not to smear it. Let paint dry.

4. Try stars, moons, or other designs cut from heavy paper, or even common household articles. Become a Cub Scout spatter printer.

To make a frame for the screen:

1. Form a square frame as illustrated. The frame should be 2″ high.

2. Use two 1½″ nails to secure each corner.

3. Tack the wire screen all around the frame.

TACK OR NAIL SECURELY.

FRAME — BOTTOM VIEW

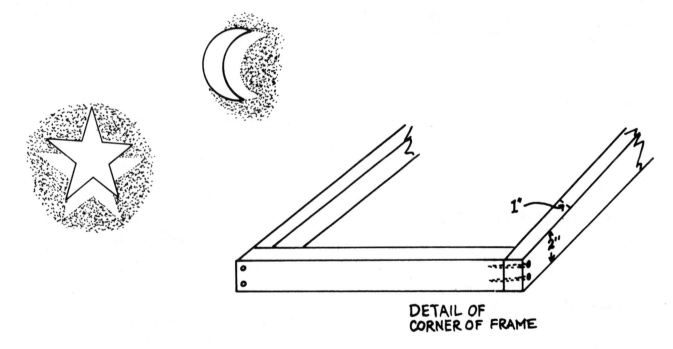

1″

2″

DETAIL OF CORNER OF FRAME

JIGSAW PUZZLE GREETING CARD

Send a jigsaw puzzle greeting card to a sick friend as a gift.

BLANK SIDE OF HEAVY PAPER

PASTE ON PICTURE AND LETTERING.

JIGSAW PUZZLE IS TRACED ON THE BACK.

SIGN YOUR NAME HERE.

HURRY UP
Get WELL SOON
Jack Jones

ADVANCEMENT POSSIBILITY

Wolf Elective 9: Let's Have a Party

MATERIALS

Paste

Scissors

Plain envelope

Sheet of heavy paper or construction paper

Old magazine

PROCEDURE

1. Cut a small colored picture about 4" × 3" high from a magazine.

2. Cut letters from magazines to spell "Hurry Up—Get Well Soon," or other greetings.

3. Paste the picture and letters on the blank side of the heavy paper, as shown here.

4. Put your card between sheets of clean paper and place under a heavy book to dry.

5. When the paste is dry, sign your name on the card. On the back side of your card, draw jigsaw puzzle shapes. Next cut the card into pieces.

6. Address an envelope then put the puzzle pieces into the envelope and mail.

SECRET CODE WHEEL

Send secret messages to a friend who knows the "key."

ADVANCEMENT POSSIBILITY

Wolf Elective 1: It's a Secret

MATERIALS

Paste

Scissors

Cardboard

Small paper brad

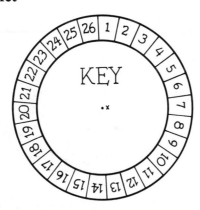

PROCEDURE

1. Draw the code wheels directly onto the cardboard.

2. Cut out the circles and place the smaller circle marked "key" on top of the larger circle.

3. Punch a small hole in the center (point X) of each wheel. Insert the paper brad. Spread the "legs" of the brad so the wheels are fairly tight against each other. The wheels should turn freely.

4. For your first message, turn the "key" circle so that the number 15 is directly under the letter A on the larger circle. At the top of your message write "A-15" which explains the key to the code. Now write your message, using corresponding numbers instead of letters. "How are you?" would be written "22-3-11 15-6-19 13-3-9."

5. On receiving your message, your buddy first sets his code wheel to "A-15" which is written on the top of your message. He then has the key for reading the coded message.

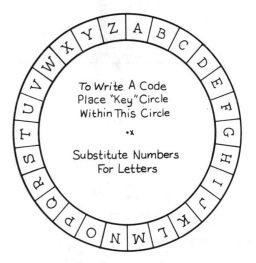

6. Twenty-six different codes can be written by using the code wheel in various combinations of letters and numbers.

Use your code wheel to read this message.

"A-13" 16-1 11-1-7-4 14-17-5-6

THE PUZZLE SHOP

Amaze and challenge your family and friends or as a gesture of goodwill, give these blocks to boys or girls in a hospital.

ADVANCEMENT POSSIBILITIES

Wolf Elective 3: Make It Yourself

Wolf Elective 9: Let's Have a Party

Webelos Craftsman Activity Badge

CLATTER BLOCKS

MATERIALS

24" strip of wood, 3" × ¼"

Cloth tape or heavy ribbon, 36" × ⅜"

Stapler with staples or small tacks

Sandpaper

PROCEDURE

1. Cut the strip into eight 3″ pieces to make the blocks. You will need six or seven, so this gives you some extras if some should split. Sand all the edges. Lay six or seven blocks end to end on a table, leaving about ¼″ space between blocks.

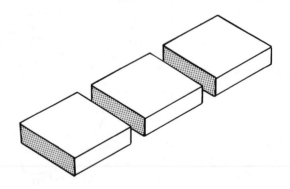

2. Next weave the two outer tapes around the blocks, stapling tape to the top end of each block as shown.

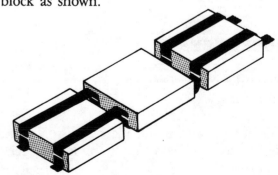

3. Then weave in the center tape through the line of blocks in reverse direction and staple to the bottom end of each block as shown.

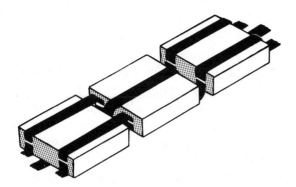

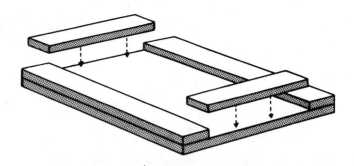

TO WORK: Hold one end block by its edges between thumb and fingertips. Start action by alternately dipping or raising the wrist and watch the amazing blocks perform.

2. To make the key block (No. 1 in diagram), glue two 2″ pieces together side by side to form a 2″ square. Sand the edges of each block so that they will slip past each other easily. Cut eight additional blocks as follows: two 1″×1″ blocks and six 2″×1″ blocks. Number each as shown in the diagram.

THE NINE-BLOCK PUZZLE

MATERIALS

A piece of furring strip 40″×1″×¼″ for sides and blocks

A piece of plywood 6″×7″ for base

Sandpaper

Tacks

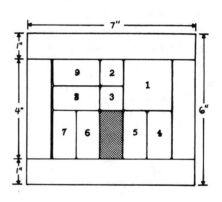

PUZZLE: To move the large block from the upper right to the lower left corner without lifting the blocks.

PROCEDURE

1. Make a shallow box with inside measurements 4″×5″. Tack narrow strips (two 7″ and two 4″) to a piece of plywood leaving just enough space to allow blocks to slide. See diagram.

SOLUTION: Move blocks in the following order: (1) 2 and 3 (2) 1 (3) 4 (4) 5 (5) 2 right of 3 (6) 1 (7) 9 (8) 8 (9) 6 and 7 (10) 2 and 3 (11) 1 (12) 9 (13) 8 (14) 6 and 7 (15) 2 above 3 (16) 1 (17) 5 (18) 4 (19) 8 and 9 (20) 6 and 7 (21) 2 and 3 (22) 1.

TRICKS

Here are a couple of tricks for you to try on your family or friends. Practice until you can do them well. For more ideas for tricks, see *Boys' Life* magazine and *Cub Scout Magic.*

ADVANCEMENT POSSIBILITY

Bear Elective 13: Magic

HINDU STRING TRICK

Show two pieces of string as illustrated in figure A. The upper ends of the strings are then placed in your mouth as shown in figure B. Using both hands, move the string several times from left to right and right to left, while the string is in your mouth. Also pretend to swallow. You then produce one long string.

Shhhhh—Here's the secret: Use a string about 36" long and another small piece of string about 4" long. Loop the small piece through the center of the large piece, as shown in illustration D. Then hold both pieces with your fingers, as shown in fig. A, hiding the loop with your fingers. When the string is placed in your mouth, use your tongue to quickly remove the short piece and let your tongue push it on the side of your lower gum. After a little "showmanship," produce the one long string, making it seem as though two short strings have become one long string.

SEE THROUGH YOUR HAND

Would you like to be able to see right through your hand? Well, with this trick you can. Roll a piece of paper into a tube and hold it as shown. Look through the tube and keep both eyes open. You'll see a hole the size of the tube in your hand.

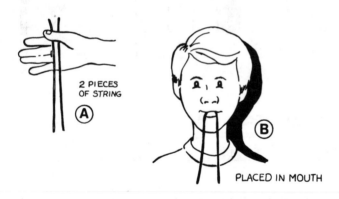

2 PIECES OF STRING (A)

PLACED IN MOUTH (B)

BECOME ONE LONG PIECE (C)

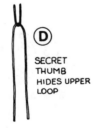

SECRET THUMB HIDES UPPER LOOP (D)

THE SEALED WORLD

Learn more about nature and how everything is dependent upon something else.

ADVANCEMENT POSSIBILITY

Webelos Naturalist Activity Badge

MATERIALS

Large, wide-mouth glass jar (1 gal. minimum)

A marshy area near the edge of a pond or stream.

Paraffin or tape

PROCEDURE

1. Put about 1½" sandy soil or sand in the bottom of the jar.

2. Plant five or six water plants in the soil.

3. Fill the jar to where the neck narrows with water from a pond. The water may look lifeless, but actually it contains plankton—tiny plants and animals. The water may take several days to clear.

4. Add a snail and two minnows not more than 1" long. Put the screw top on the jar and seal it with paraffin or tape.

NOTE: Keep the jar where it will get *indirect sunlight,* so that the water does not get warmed by the sun. With no further attention, the sealed world should sustain itself almost indefinitely.

What is happening? The green plants use light, minerals from the soil, water, and the carbon dioxide exhaled by the fish and snail. The plants exhale oxygen that is needed by the plankton, fish, and snail. The fish eat the plankton, but the tiny plankton keep multiplying so fast that the food supply will last a long time. The snail eats plankton, too, but is a scavenger that also feeds on tiny plants growing on larger plants and the glass. In this way, a balance is struck in the sealed world which may continue for a long time.

SMALL GREENHOUSE

Learn to grow and care for plants by making a terrarium. It is a little garden sealed in a glass container. Rich soil and moisture inside the jar make the garden grow quickly. In planting your garden, use wild ferns, violets, moss, and small cuttings of ivy or any houseplant that will grow in water.

ADVANCEMENT POSSIBILITIES

Wolf Elective 15: Grow Something

Webelos Naturalist Activity Badge

MATERIALS

A clear, wide-mouth, 1-gal. glass or plastic jar and lid (ask at your neighborhood grocery, restaurant, or delicatessen for an empty pickle jar)

Sand or bird gravel

A piece of burned wood or some charcoal

About 2 c. of rich garden soil

Plywood, 12" × 8"

Strips of wood ½" thick and 1" wide

Thin brads or nails

Hammer

Saw

Paint or stain, if desired

Sandpaper

Variety of small plants

BUILD THE BASE FOR THE GARDEN

1. Five pieces of wood are used to make the base, as pictured. Sandpaper the inside edges of the frame to make the jar fit snugly within it.

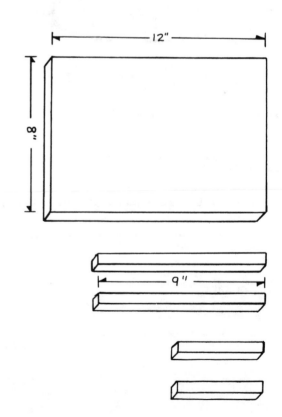

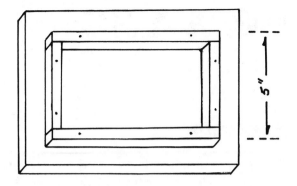

9. Watch the garden carefully for a day or two. If it appears to be too wet, take off the jar lid for a day or more until the garden dries some.

10. The garden will grow for 2 or 3 months without having to be opened.

PLANT YOUR GARDEN INSIDE THE JAR

2. Place the jar, thoroughly clean, on its side on the wooden base.

3. Put a ½" layer of sand or bird gravel in the bottom of the jar as it lies on its side.

4. Crush a piece of charcoal or burned wood between newspapers and sprinkle a layer of charcoal over the sand.

5. Add a layer of rich dirt. The garden can be higher at the back side of the jar, but be sure the dirt is smoothed away from the mouth of the jar so that it will not spill out.

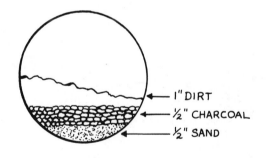

6. Set your plants at least an inch deep in the soil.

7. Spray the garden with water. Do not get the dirt too wet.

8. Seal the jar with the lid and set the tiny greenhouse in a spot where it will get some sunlight each day.

TRY GROWING OTHER THINGS IN WATER

Place the top inch of a carrot in a small bowl of water and watch it sprout. Try this also with sweet potato, pineapple top, or avocado seed. For the potato and avocado, stick toothpicks in at three places to hold them partly above the water.

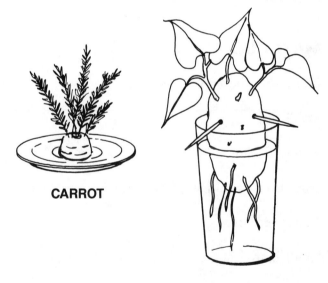

CARROT

SWEET POTATO

A WEATHER VANE

Use this as wind-direction indicator to predict weather conditions.

ADVANCEMENT POSSIBILITY

Bear Elective 2: Weather

MATERIALS

Broom handle or 1" dowel rod

Small nut

Some 4d nails

Stick from an old window shade

Adhesive tape

Small brads

No. 2 tin can, or a piece of tin

Tin snips or heavy scissors

Pieces of scrap wood

Hammer

Saw

Pliers

PROCEDURE

The jig is a wooden frame used for holding the window-shade stick as you work with it. The jig takes only a few minutes to make, but it will save much time in making the weather vane.

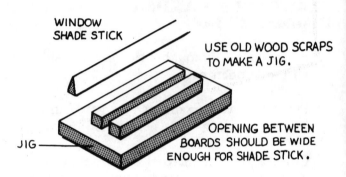

1. Mark a line 8" from the rivet in the center of the window-shade stick. Now set the stick in the jig and saw the stick in two at the pencil mark.

2. Measure 12" from the rivet on the other end of the window-shade stick and saw the stick in two at the point.

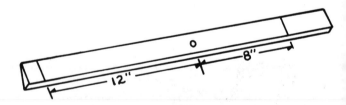

3. With a knife, sharpen the 12" side of the stick into a blunt point.

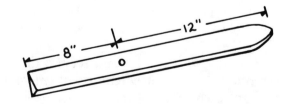

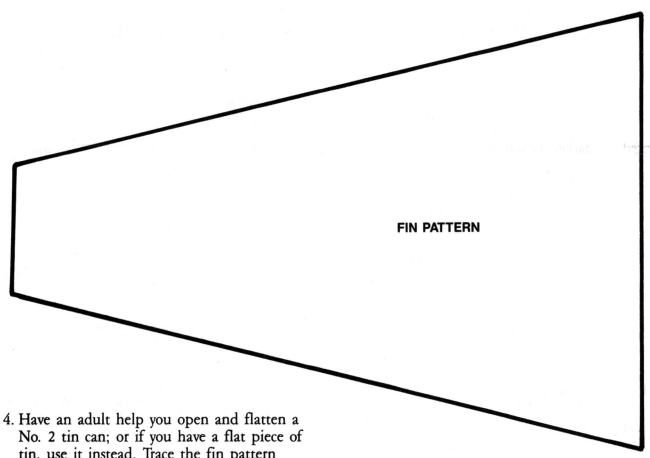

FIN PATTERN

4. Have an adult help you open and flatten a No. 2 tin can; or if you have a flat piece of tin, use it instead. Trace the fin pattern (shown here) on the tin and cut it out with a pair of tin snips or heavy scissors. Use pliers to turn up a very narrow edge along the slanting sides of the fin, then hammer the edges down flat.

5. Place the window-shade stick in the jig with the wide edge of the stick on top. Center the fin on the 8″ end of the stick and nail it fast. Use very small (No. 8) brads or nails, or the wood might split.

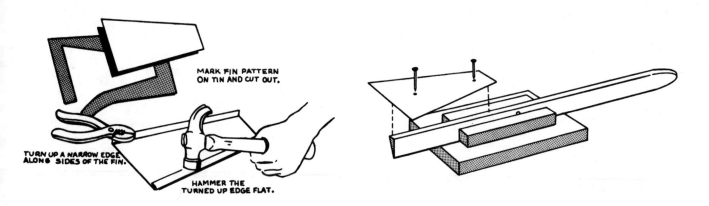

MARK FIN PATTERN ON TIN AND CUT OUT.

TURN UP A NARROW EDGE ALONG SIDES OF THE FIN.

HAMMER THE TURNED UP EDGE FLAT.

6. At the 12″ end of the stick, tape enough small nails to the narrow edge to balance the stick as pictured.

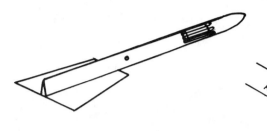

7. Sharpen one end of the broomstick so it can be driven into the ground. Then fold a "tin flag" around a broadhead nail. Nail the flag to the broomstick, 4″ from the flat end. The flag on the broomstick is to be your "true north" indicator.

8. Select a good spot in your yard for the weather vane. Drive the broomstick into the ground so the flag points directly to the North Star. On sunny days, at noon, the shadow of the broomstick will also point "true north."

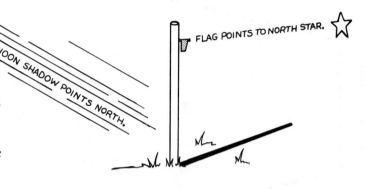

9. Put a fourpenny nail through the rivet in the wind vane, then slip a small nut over the end of the nail and hammer the nail into the top of the broomstick.

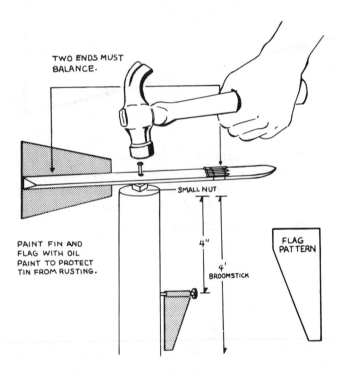

RAIN GAUGE

Measure the rainfall where you live. Keep a record for one week or longer.

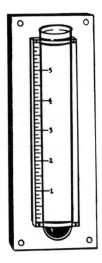

MATERIALS

A test tube or glass cigar tube

Block of wood about 8" long

6" ruler

Bands of tin or wire

Clay or sealing wax

Drill with ¼" bit

Two small nails

Four small screws

Hammer

PROCEDURE

1. Drill small holes in each corner of the wooden block.

2. Fill the rounded bottom of the test tube with clay or sealing wax. This levels off the bottom and permits accurate measurement of water.

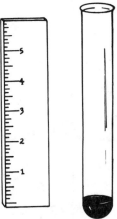

3. Nail ruler to center of the block.

4. With wire or tin bands, attach test tube against the ruler, so that clay or wax in bottom of the tube lies at the tip of the ruler on the lower end of the block.

5. Fasten the rain gauge to a fence or post, in an open area, away from buildings or trees. After each rain, read the gauge to see how much water fell, then empty the tube and set back into place.

TIN CAN BIRD FEEDER

Put this feeder in your backyard or on your porch to attract birds.

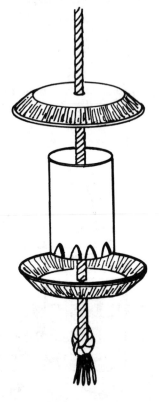

ADVANCEMENT POSSIBILITY

Wolf Elective 13: Birds

MATERIALS

Large juice can (with top removed)

Bright colored enamel paint and paintbrush

Two aluminum pie tins

3' of clothesline rope

Hammer

Large nail

Beverage can opener

PROCEDURE

1. Paint the juice can in the color of your choice. When it is dry, punch a hole through the middle of the bottom of the can, using the hammer and nail.

2. Punch a series of openings around bottom of can using the beverage can opener. This is where the birdseed comes out.

3. Punch holes in the middle of the two pie tins, using the large nail and hammer.

4. Now, tie a knot in the end of the clothesline and run the rope up through one pie tin, the juice can, and finally the other pie tin. See illustration for details.

5. Fill can with birdseed and hang in your yard or on an open porch.

6. Enjoy the birds that come to visit.

BUILD A BUG HOUSE

Learn about insects by building an insect "zoo."

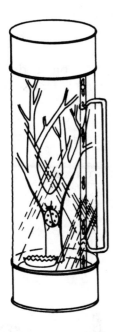

ADVANCEMENT POSSIBILITY

Webelos Naturalist Activity Badge

MATERIALS

Two tuna or cat food cans

Screen wire 10" x 10"

Two metal paper fasteners

Plaster or caulking

Enamel paint

Bottle cap

Twig

Wire for handle (use coathanger)

Paintbrush

PROCEDURE

1. Form screen into a 10" long cylinder, overlapping sides. Secure with paper fasteners.

2. Paint cans with enamel paint. If you wish, you may paint a design on the lid. Let paint dry.

3. Fill bottom can half full of plaster or calking. Before it hardens, stick in a twig (for bugs to crawl on) and bottle cap (to hold water).

4. Insert screen wire cylinder into plaster and let harden.

5. Attach wire handles to sides of the screen. Set lid (other can) on top of wire cylinder. The lid is not attached so it can be easily removed.

6. Now find a bug for your "bug house." Don't forget to feed and water your pet.

WOODEN BIRD FEEDERS

Attract birds to your backyard or porch in winter.

BIRD FEEDER NO. 1

1. Put a screw eye in the top center of a 10" log.

2. Use a brace and ¾" bit to drill four holes, ½" deep, as pictured. Holes should be staggered.

3. Holes slant downward.

4. Hang feeder from a tree with wire and fill with birdseed.

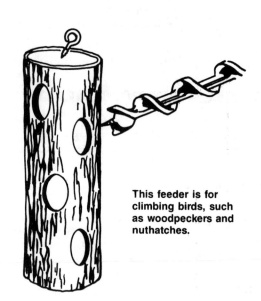

This feeder is for climbing birds, such as woodpeckers and nuthatches.

ADVANCEMENT POSSIBILITY

Wolf Elective 13: Birds

MATERIALS

Three large screw eyes

Piece of wire

Brace and bits to drill ¼" and ¾" holes

Small log about 10" long

¼" dowel or small sticks

2"×4" piece of wood 10" long

Some evergreen twigs

BIRD FEEDER NO. 2

1. Put two screw eyes in the top of a 10″ piece of 2×4 wood.

2. Drill four holes, ½″ deep, ¾″ wide, as pictured.

3. One inch below each food hole, drill a ¼″ hole for a perch.

4. Drill ¼″ holes in both sides, and insert evergreen twigs for extra attraction to the birds.

5. Food holes and perch holes slant downward.

6. Perches are made of dowel sticks, or from straight twigs.

7. Hang feeder from a tree and fill with birdseed.

Birds like a variety of seeds. To attract the most variety, use different types of feeders and a good mix of birdseed. In winter be sure to keep the feeders full.

MILK CARTON BIRD FEEDER

Attract birds to your yard by feeding them, especially during the winter.

Steel square or ruler

Sharp knife or razor blade

Sharp pencil

Two 6" wood dowels

Hole punch or awl

PROCEDURE

1. Using a steel square, cut carton as shown on opposite sides with sharp blade. Cut 2¼" from bottom, 1¼" from top.

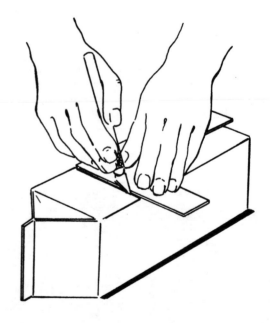

ADVANCEMENT POSSIBILITY

Wolf Elective 13: Birds

MATERIALS
(This makes two feeders)

Three ½-gal. plastic-coated milk cartons

Stapler and staples

2. Cut opposite corners to form flaps, fold them, and staple to side panels. Fold and staple spout shut.

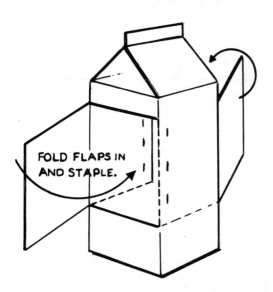

3. Using a cardboard pattern for a guide, mark center of hole on each side for the perch. Holes may be punched first, then enlarged to correct size with sharp pencil. Remove top and bottom from a third carton, cut apart on opposite corners to make roofs.

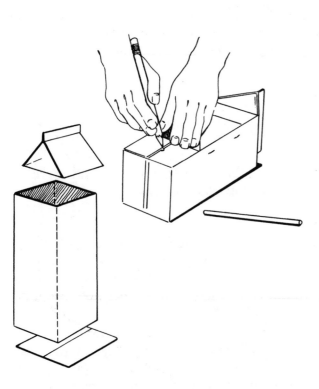

4. Fold each roof section and cut ends to size. Now, working from center fold, use a ruler as a guide and score ridge folds with a blunt point. Attach roof to body with staples, then put ⅛" hole in ridge center so feeder can hang on limb.

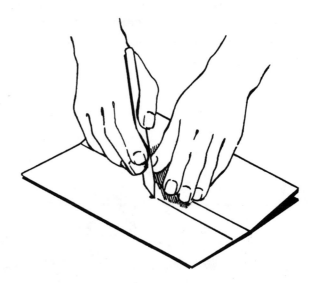

5. Finished feeders may be hung from a tree limb or fastened on top of a post. Fill with wild birdseed.

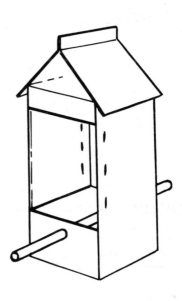

WATERSCOPE

You can explore the wonders of the underwater world, watch the movement of fish, or study aquatic rocks and plants.

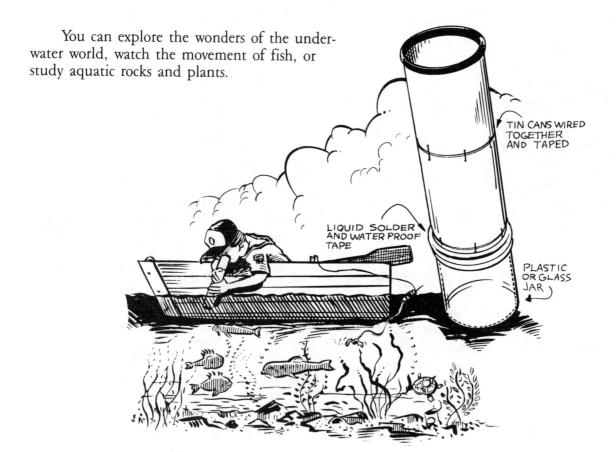

TIN CANS WIRED TOGETHER AND TAPED

LIQUID SOLDER AND WATER PROOF TAPE

PLASTIC OR GLASS JAR

ADVANCEMENT POSSIBILITY

Webelos Naturalist Activity Badge

MATERIALS

Three large fruit-juice cans all same-size

1" wide waterproof adhesive tape

Glass jar slightly wider than juice cans

Wire

PROCEDURE

1. Remove both ends from all three cans.

2. Place the cans end-to-end and align the seams. Fasten with wire and 1" wide waterproof adhesive tape.

3. Insert this cylinder into a jar and make the joint watertight with waterproof adhesive tape.

By eliminating surface reflections, the waterscope allows you to see directly under water. Be sure you have good footing on the dock, rock ledge, or rowboat before leaning over the water.

NOTE: Carefully check the edge of the can that will be against your face for jagged edges. Use a metal file to make rough edges smooth. For an added precaution, apply duct tape to cover this same edge.

BURROMETER

Make a just-for-fun weather forecaster!

MATERIALS

Cardboard

Construction paper

String or colored yarn

PROCEDURE

Trace or enlarge the drawing in this book. Add letters and a tail. If you are going to hang your burrometer outside, cover the cardboard with plastic before adding the tail.

BURROMETER

If tail is dry	FAIR
If tail is wet	RAIN
If tail is swinging	WINDY
If tail is wet & swinging	STORMY
If tail is frozen	COLD
If tail is gone	TORNADO

ANT FARM

Study how ants work underground.

ADVANCEMENT POSSIBILITY

Webelos Naturalist Activity Badge

MATERIALS

1-gal. jar (ask for a pickle jar at a restaurant or delicatessen)

Can that fits inside the jar

Soil

Small flat dish (just a little bigger than the top of the can)

Wooden block

Large pan

Cheesecloth or screen

Dark paper

Rubber bands

Trowel

White cloth or paper about 2' square

Piece of cardboard

Two large-mouth bottles or jars with lids

PROCEDURE

1. Fill jar about half full of the slightly moist soil. Place the can an inch or two into the soil, and place the small flat dish on the can. (See illustration.) Now, you are ready to hunt for your ants.

3. Carry some soil from the ant nest back with you and put it into your nest (not into the can). Fill most of the space left between the jar and the can. Put the ants and queen into the nest and close jar with a cheesecloth or screen. Fasten dark paper around the jar with rubber bands. Ants like the dark. They will build their tunnels close to the glass, where you can observe them. Place the jar on a wood block in a pan of water as shown. This will prevent the ants from escaping.

4. Feed the ants by putting different kinds of food on top of the soil. Try bread, cake crumbs, bits of meat, honey, small pieces of vegetables, or dead insects. Always remove unused food before adding new food. Keep the dish on top of the can filled with water. If soil gets very dry, moisten it a little with an eyedropper.

5. Place the jar in a warm place, but not in direct sunlight. After a couple of days, the ants will have settled down.

6. Watch the tunnel building, egg and larvae moving. Try some experiments. Take some ants out of the nest for a few days then put them back in and see what happens. Introduce some new ants from outdoors and see what happens. Set up regular feeding time and see how soon they learn when it is. Keep the jar covered when not observing your new pets because ants work only in the dark.

2. Find an anthill or an ant nest under some rocks. Stir it up with your trowel and as the ants come out to investigate, guide them into one of the bottles with the cardboard. After you have collected about a hundred, screw the cap back on. Now, you need to find the queen and this requires some digging. You may have to dig as much as a foot to find the queen. Take the dirt you dig and spread it out on the white cloth or paper. One ant larger than the rest will probably show up against the white background. This is the queen. It is best to guide her into the second bottle and close it quickly so that you don't lose her.

MAKE WATER RISE INTO A GLASS

Test the air and water pressure and amaze your friends or family with this science trick.

ADVANCEMENT POSSIBILITIES

Bear Elective 13: Magic

Webelos Scientist Activity Badge

MATERIALS

Plate

Match

Water glass

Scrap of paper

Small piece of cardboard

PROCEDURE

1. Pour a little water on a plate.

2. Float a small piece of heavy cardboard on the water and place a scrap of newspaper on the cardboard.

3. Light the scrap of newspaper and quickly cover the flame with a glass.

4. As the fire goes out, water will rise slowly into the glass.

THIS IS WHAT HAPPENS

It is fun to think a battle is taking place when water rises into the glass. It really is a battle between fire, water, and air.

When you set the glass over fire, a glassful of air—which we shall call inside air—is trapped in the glass with the fire. Water around the rim of the glass locks (or seals) the fire and inside air in the glass.

As the fire burns, it heats the inside air. Therefore, the inside air begins to expand, and some of it is forced out through the water.

The fire uses oxygen as it burns, and goes out when the oxygen is gone. After the fire is out, the inside air cools and contracts, but now there is less of it. The inside air pressure goes down.

Outside air—the air outside the glass—tries to rush into the glass to fill the low-pressure area, but water is in its way. Pushed by outside air, water is forced up into the glass to fill the low-pressure area.

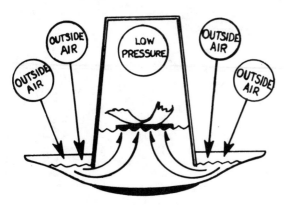

When the fire has used all the oxygen in the inside air, the battle is over. The fire dies. Water rises inside the glass. Outside air is the winner.

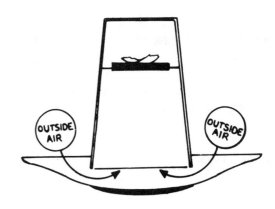

NOTE: Be sure to have an adult present when you try this experiment.

MAKE ELECTRICITY

By rubbing two unlike objects together, you can produce a type of electricity known as static electricity. It will not shock you or hurt you. By doing the four experiments on this page, you will learn some of the ways that static electricity is produced.

MATERIALS

Comb

Sheet of typing paper

Playing card (not plastic)

Piece of tissue paper or cleansing tissue

PROCEDURE

1. Rub a playing card rapidly back and forth on a wool sweater or jacket. Press the card against the wall. If the wallpaper is not too slick or oily, the card will stick there.

2. Rub a piece of typing paper quickly back and forth on the wall. The typing paper will stick to the wall.

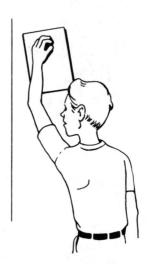

3. Comb your hair briskly with a dry comb. Hold the comb close to your hair and see how the static electricity draws the ends of the hair to the comb. If your hair is wet or oily, this experiment will not work.

4. Briskly comb your hair with a dry comb and touch it to a small piece of tissue paper. The tissue paper will stick to the comb.

HOW STRONG IS AIR?

Test the strength of air around you and amaze your friends with a trick.

ADVANCEMENT POSSIBILITIES

Bear Elective 13: Magic

Webelos Scientist Activity Badge

MATERIALS

Glass

Several squares of lightweight cardboard

PROCEDURE

1. Fill a glass with water. Place cardboard on top of the glass.

2. Turn glass upside down, then let go of cardboard. The air pressing against the cardboard holds water in the glass.

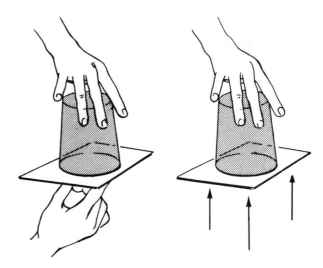

3. Air will hold water in the glass, no matter which way you turn the glass. Air exerts strength in all directions—up, down, and to all sides.

4. It still works when the glass is only half full of water.

5. When the glass is empty, the cardboard falls. Why? Because the air inside the glass has as much strength as the air outside the glass. Therefore, the cardboard yields to the pull of gravity.

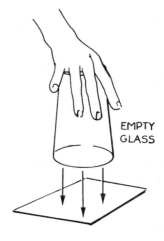

NOTE: Work at the sink, so that spilling water won't matter.

THE THREE-IN-ONE STORYTELLER

PROCEDURE

1. When the Cub Scout speaks, put on the Cub Scout cap and speak in your natural voice.

2. When the den chief speaks, put on the Boy Scout cap and speak in a deeper voice.

3. When the den leader speaks, put on the leader's cap and speak in a very deep voice.

4. The story is funnier when you change hats quickly and speak rapidly. But be sure to speak clearly so that everyone can understand what you are saying.

5. Memorize the story. It isn't very long.

6. Stand behind a low table as you tell the story. Place the hats on the table in front of you.

THE STORY

"Ladies and gentlemen, three Cub Scouts were going to present a play for you tonight, but the other two boys haven't come. Therefore, I will have to play all the parts myself. The name of the play is *Cub Scout Inspection*. The cast of characters is the den leader, the den chief, and a Cub Scout named Johnny, wearing one red and one blue sock. The scene is a Cub Scout den meeting. The den leader is speaking:"

CUB SCOUT

DEN LEADER

DEN CHIEF

DEN LEADER: Cub Scouts, line up for inspection.

DEN CHIEF: They all look fine, except Johnny.

JOHNNY: Me?

DEN LEADER: Johnny?

DEN CHIEF: Yes, Johnny?

JOHNNY: What's wrong with me?

DEN LEADER: What's wrong with him?

DEN CHIEF: Look at his socks.

JOHNNY: My socks?

DEN LEADER: His socks?

DEN CHIEF: Your socks.

DEN LEADER: Why Johnny, you have on one red sock . . .

DEN CHIEF: . . . and one blue sock.

JOHNNY: One red sock?

DEN CHIEF: Yes, and one blue sock.

JOHNNY: That's funny.

DEN CHIEF: What's funny?

DEN LEADER: What's funny?

JOHNNY: I have another pair just like them at home.

THE END

STICK PUPPETS

Present a puppet play to your family or friends, or help your den put on a skit at pack meeting.

ADVANCEMENT POSSIBILITY

Webelos Showman Activity Badge

MATERIALS

Paste

Scissors

Thumbtacks or strong glue

Four thin strips of wood about 12" long

Cardboard

Crayons or paint

Sandpaper

PROCEDURE

1. Draw or trace puppet figures from a book and then paste on lightweight cardboard. Your puppets can be animals, people, or space creatures.

2. Color or paint the puppets and cut them out.

3. Cut four strips of wood about ½" wide and 12" long from a piece of soft wood. Sandpaper until smooth.

4. With thumbtacks or strong glue, fasten each puppet to a strip of wood.

You are now ready to put on your puppet play. Puppet characters can be made from your own drawings, or from pictures in magazines or coloring books.

CUB SCOUT CHEF

It is fun to prepare food in the kitchen and on campouts or other outings. Here are some easy recipes to try. Be sure an adult is present when you use the stove or grill.

ADVANCEMENT POSSIBILITIES

Wolf Achievement 8: Cooking and Eating

Bear Achievement 9: What's Cooking

Webelos Outdoorsman Activity Badge

WIENER KABOBS

Wieners

Pineapple chunks

Alternate wiener pieces and pineapple chunks on a skewer. Broil on grill or over coals until wieners are hot.

STUFFED HOT DOG

Wiener

Slice of bacon

Toothpick

Slice of cheese

Choice of pickles, sauerkraut, or onions, if desired.

Slice the wiener lengthwise, but not all the way through. Stuff the middle with stuffings of your choice, then twist bacon around the wiener and secure it with a toothpick. Grill until bacon is done, turning several times.

S'MORES

Everybody always wants s'mores!

Graham crackers

Milk chocolate candy bar

Marshmallows

Place four squares of chocolate bar on graham cracker. Put a hot toasted marshmallow on top of the chocolate and another graham cracker on top of the marshmallow. You can also use chocolate-covered grahams—without the candy bar.

YODEL YIPPERS

(This is an unbaked cookie.)

1½ c. quick oatmeal

¼ c. peanut butter

¼ c. milk

½ tsp. vanilla

1 c. sugar

¼ c. margarine

¼ c. cocoa powder (unsweetened)

Combine oatmeal and peanut butter in bowl until a coarse mixture is obtained.

Heat the other ingredients gently in a sauce pan, stirring constantly. Allow it to boil 1 minute, then remove from heat.

Pour this liquid mixture into the oatmeal and peanut butter and stir. Use a teaspoon and a knife to drop spoonsful onto a sheet of waxed paper. The "Yodel Yippers" are ready as soon as they cool. Makes about 2 dozen cookies.

TANGY HAM

A good item for dinner at a campout with your family.

¼ c. orange marmalade

2 tbsp. of soy sauce

Slices of precooked ham

Mix the orange marmalade and soy sauce. Spread sauce on both sides of a slice of ham and grill for 5 minutes on each side.

ONE-DISH BREAKFAST

2 slices of bacon

1 slice bread

1 egg

Salt and pepper (to taste)

Fry bacon on griddle until almost cooked. Tear a hole from the middle of the bread, then place over bacon slices. Break egg into hole in bread and cook until egg is done.

NOTES

NOTES

NOTES

NOTES

NOTES

NOTES

NOTES

NOTES